FREE VIDEO  **FREE VIDEO**

ACT WorkKeys® Essential Test Tips Video from Trivium Test Prep!

Dear Customer,

Thank you for purchasing from Trivium Test Prep! We're honored to help you prepare for your ACT WorkKeys® exam.

To show our appreciation, we're offering a **FREE *ACT WorkKeys® Essential Test Tips* Video by Trivium Test Prep**.* Our video includes 35 test preparation strategies that will make you successful on the ACT WorkKeys®. All we ask is that you email us your feedback and describe your experience with our product. Amazing, awful, or just so-so: we want to hear what you have to say!

To receive your **FREE *ACT WorkKeys® Essential Test Tips* Video**, please email us at 5star@ triviumtestprep.com. Include "Free 5 Star" in the subject line and the following information in your email:

1. The title of the product you purchased.

2. Your rating from 1 – 5 (with 5 being the best).

3. Your feedback about the product, including how our materials helped you meet your goals and ways in which we can improve our products.

4. Your full name and shipping address so we can send your **FREE *ACT WorkKeys® Essential Test Tips* Video**.

If you have any questions or concerns please feel free to contact us directly at 5star@ triviumtestprep.com.

Thank you!

- Trivium Test Prep Team

*To get access to the free video please email us at 5star@triviumtestprep.com, and please follow the instructions above.

WorkKeys® Study Guide and Practice Test Questions

ACT WorkKeys® Exam Prep and Review Book with Applied Mathematics, Locating Information, and Reading for Information

TABLE OF CONTENTS

ONLINE RESOURCES

To help you fully prepare for your ACT WorkKeys® exam, Trivium includes online resources with the purchase of this study guide.

Practice Test

In addition to the practice test included in this book, we also offer an online exam. Since many exams today are computer based, getting to practice your test-taking skills on the computer is a great way to prepare.

Flash Cards

A convenient supplement to this study guide, Trivium's flash cards enable you to review important terms easily on your computer or smartphone.

Cheat Sheets

Review the core skills you need to master the exam with easy-to-read Cheat Sheets.

From Stress to Success

Watch "From Stress to Success," a brief but insightful YouTube video that offers the tips, tricks, and secrets experts use to score higher on the exam.

Reviews

Leave a review, send us helpful feedback, or sign up for Trivium promotions—including free books!

Access these materials at:

www.triviumtestprep.com/act-workkeys-online-resources

INTRODUCTION

Congratulations on choosing to take the ACT WorkKeys® Assessments! By purchasing this book, you've taken an important step on your path to joining the workforce or climbing the corporate ladder.

This guide will provide you with a detailed overview of the ACT WorkKeys® so that you know exactly what to expect on test day. We'll take you through all the concepts covered on the assessments and give you the opportunity to test your knowledge with practice questions. Even if it's been a while since you last took a major test, don't worry; we'll make sure you're more than ready!

WHAT ARE THE ACT WORKKEYS® ASSESSMENTS?

The ACT WorkKeys® Assessments measure a candidate's readiness to enter the workforce. The ACT WorkKeys® is not one single test: it is made up of several assessments. Candidates can take as few or as many of the assessments as they wish. The most important assessments are the **APPLIED MATH**, **GRAPHIC LITERACY**, and **WORKPLACE DOCUMENTS** assessments.

Why take the ACT WorkKeys®? First of all, high-school students in eight states are required to take it. At least thirty states use the ACT WorkKeys® in workforce development programs. Seventeen states that participate in the ACT's Certified Work Ready Communities initiative use it, and many employers throughout the nation require it. Finally, state programs and employers use the ACT WorkKeys® to determine candidates' readiness for employment and gauge their skills.

What is the NCRC?

The candidate who successfully completes the Applied Math, Graphic Literacy, and Workplace Documents assessments will receive the **WORKKEYS® NATIONAL CAREER READINESS CERTIFICATE (NCRC)**. There are four levels of NCRC: Platinum, Gold, Silver, and Bronze. To earn your NCRC, you must complete all three assessments with a level of 3 or above.

The NCRC certifies that a candidate has a certain level of skill or potential for success in various jobs. An NCRC shows employers that you are ready to take on the responsibilities of your position. More and more employers around the nation are requiring the NCRC. An NCRC can also help you earn college or continuing education credit.

WHAT'S ON THE ACT WORKKEYS®?

Three assessments are required to earn the NCRC: Applied Math, Graphic Literacy, and Workplace Documents. They are each composed of multiple-choice questions with four or five answer choices.

What's on the ACT WorkKeys®?

ASSESSMENT	TOPICS	NUMBER OF QUESTIONS	TIME
Applied Math	■ Solve problems using mathematical operations (addition, subtraction, multiplication, division) ■ Complete problems using decimals, percentages, and fractions ■ Understand ratios, proportions, and rates ■ Convert among various units of measurement ■ Calculate area, perimeter, circumference, and volume ■ Use graphics, percentage difference, or unit cost ■ Apply statistical and data analysis concepts	34	55 minutes
Graphic Literacy	■ Read and locate information presented graphically (tables, graphs, flowcharts, infographics) ■ Compare information among graphics ■ Identify and interpret trends, patterns, and relationships ■ Apply information and inferences from one graphic or part of the graphic to another graphic ■ Justify a decision or inference based on information in the graphic	38	55 minutes
Workplace Documents	■ Read and understand informative materials, company policies and procedures, memos, and instructional documents ■ Identify the main idea and supporting ideas in the passage ■ Draw inferences or conclusions from the text, including when to follow certain procedures in specific situations ■ Understand or infer vocabulary in context ■ Apply information and inferences from one part of the reading to other parts	35	55 minutes
Total		107	2 hours and 45 minutes

The **APPLIED MATH** assessment tests your ability to perform arithmetic and mathematical operations, including solving operations with fractions, decimals, percentages, ratios, and proportions; finding area, perimeter, circumference, and volume; converting among measurements; and evaluating graphic data. Prepare for questions about using math in employment situations: for instance, making change, finding averages, budgeting, or measuring. You will have fifty-five minutes to answer thirty-four Applied Math questions.

The **GRAPHIC LITERACY** assessment tests your ability to read and understand information presented in tables, charts, diagrams, graphs, and other visual means. You will be asked to read and answer questions about bar charts, pie charts, tables of information, tables of contents, and other infographics. Questions will ask about information in the graphic or offer specific scenarios where you must use information in the graphic to solve a problem or draw a conclusion. You will have fifty-five minutes to answer thirty-eight Graphic Literacy questions.

The **WORKPLACE DOCUMENTS** assessment asks you to read documents like those you might find in a typical workplace. You will receive examples of memos, directions, policies, and other informative texts. Questions will ask you to identify key details and information, follow directions, understand the main idea or point of the passage, draw conclusions and inferences, define vocabulary in context, and understand the purpose of a document. You will have fifty-five minutes to answer thirty-five Workplace Documents questions.

HOW IS THE ACT WORKKEYS® SCORED?

You will be able to view your scores online, via your ACT WorkKeys® NCRC account at www. myworkkeys.com, after you take the exam. You will also receive an Individual Summary Score Report, which will contain a detailed explanation of your scores.

There are two important scores on your score report: your Level Score and your Scale Score. Your **LEVEL SCORE** will range from 3 – 7. This is the most important score used in hiring decisions. A score of 3 demonstrates minimum proficiency in each assessment. A score of 7 indicates a candidate has the ability to engage in complex reasoning and applied knowledge. To earn your NCRC, you need a Level Score of at least 3 on each of the three required assessments. However, different jobs may have different requirements for the assessments. You should check with your program or community college to determine your target Level Score for each assessment.

The **SCALE SCORE** is used for training purposes and is not generally used in employment decisions. It ranges from 65 – 90.

HOW IS THE ACT WORKKEYS® ADMINISTERED?

The ACT WorkKeys® is administered at testing sites around the nation. It is available as a computer-administered test or in a pencil-and-paper format, depending on the test site. Check with your test site for details. To register, you must set up an account at http://myworkkeys.com.

On test day, arrive early. Check with the facility to make sure you know what type of identification to bring (usually government-issued photo identification). Bring at least two sharpened No. 2 pencils. Personal belongings, cell phones, and other electronic, photographic, recording, or listening devices are not permitted in the testing center. Many testing centers offer lockers to secure your personal items, but you should check with the facility beforehand to find out if storage is available.

ABOUT THIS GUIDE

This guide will help you master the most important test topics and develop critical test-taking skills. We have built features into our books to prepare you for your tests and increase your score. Along with a detailed summary of the test's format, content, and scoring, we offer an in-depth overview of the content knowledge required to pass the assessments and earn your NCRC. In the review, you'll find sidebars that provide interesting information, highlight key concepts, and review content so that you can solidify your understanding of important concepts. You can also test your knowledge with sample questions throughout the text and with practice questions. We're pleased you've chosen Trivium to be a part of your journey!

APPLIED MATHEMATICS

THE MOST COMMON MISTAKES

People make little mistakes all the time, but during a test those tiny mistakes can make the difference between a good score and a poor one. Watch out for these common mistakes that people make on the Applied Mathematics Assessment of the ACT WorkKeys®:

- answering with the wrong sign (positive/negative)
- mixing up the order of operations
- misplacing a decimal
- providing an answer that was not asked for
- circling the wrong letter or filling in the wrong circle choice

If you're thinking, *those ideas are just common sense*, that's exactly the point. Most of the mistakes made on Applied Math are simple ones. But no matter how silly the mistake, a wrong answer still means a lost point on the test.

STRATEGIES FOR THE MATHEMATICS SECTION

Go Back to the Basics

First and foremost, practice your basic skills: sign changes, order of operations, simplifying fractions, and equation manipulation. These are the skills used most on Applied Math, though they are applied in many different contexts. Remember that when it comes down to it, all math problems rely on the four basic skills of addition, subtraction, multiplication, and division. All you need to figure out is the order in which they're used to solve a problem.

When working multiple-choice word problems, it's important to check your answer. Many of the incorrect choices will be answers that examinees arrive at by making common mistakes. So even if you see your answer as an answer choice, check your own work to make sure.

Don't Rely on Mental Math

Using mental math is great for eliminating answer choices, but ALWAYS WRITE DOWN YOUR WORK! This cannot be stressed enough. Use whatever paper is provided; by writing and/or drawing out the problem, you are more likely to catch any mistakes. The act of writing things down also forces you to organize your calculations, leading to an improvement in your score.

The Three-Times Rule

You should read each question at least three times to ensure you're using the correct information and answering the right question:

STEP ONE: Read the question and write out the given information.

STEP TWO: Read the question, set up your equation(s), and solve.

STEP THREE: Read the question and check that your answer makes sense (is the amount too large or small; is the answer in the correct unit of measure, etc.).

Make an Educated Guess

Eliminate those answer choices that you are relatively sure are incorrect, and then guess from the remaining choices. Educated guessing is critical to increasing your score.

TYPES OF NUMBERS

Numbers can be categorized based on their properties. While the Applied Mathematics Assessment of the ACT WorkKeys® won't directly test you on the types of numbers, it can be helpful to understand these categories while you review mathematical terms and operations.

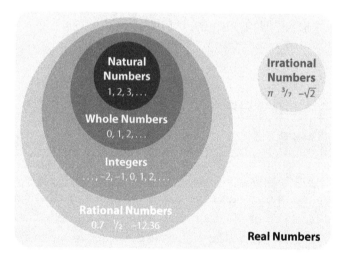

Figure 1.1. Types of Numbers

- A NATURAL NUMBER is greater than 0 and has no decimal or fraction attached. These are also sometimes called counting numbers. {1, 2, 3, 4, ...}

- WHOLE NUMBERS are natural numbers and the number 0. {0, 1, 2, 3, 4, ...}

- **INTEGERS** include positive and negative natural numbers and 0. {..., –4, –3, –2, –1, 0, 1, 2, 3, 4, ...}

- A **RATIONAL NUMBER** can be represented as a fraction. Any decimal part must terminate or resolve into a repeating pattern. (Examples: 0.7, $\frac{1}{2}$, –12.36)

- An **IRRATIONAL NUMBER** cannot be represented as a fraction. An irrational decimal number never ends and never resolves into a repeating pattern. (Examples: π, $\frac{3}{7}$, $-\sqrt{2}$)

- A **REAL NUMBER** is a number that can be represented by a point on a number line. Real numbers include all the rational and irrational numbers.

POSITIVE AND NEGATIVE NUMBERS

You can use a number line to easily find the result when adding and subtracting positive and negative numbers. When adding two numbers, whether they are positive or negative, count to the right; when subtracting, count to the left. Note that adding a negative value is the same as subtracting. Subtracting a negative value is the same as adding.

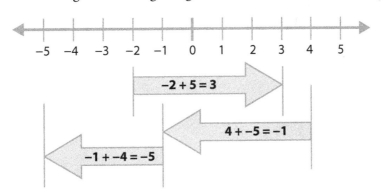

Figure 1.2. Adding and Subtracting Positive and Negative Numbers

Multiplying and dividing with negative and positive numbers is somewhat easier. Multiplying two numbers with the same sign gives a positive result, and multiplying two numbers with different signs gives a negative result. The same rules apply to division. These rules are summarized below:

(+) + (–) = the sign of the larger number

(–) + (–) = negative number

(–) × (–) or (–) ÷ (–) = positive number

(–) × (+) or (–) ÷ (+) = negative number

(+) + (+) or (+) × (+) or (+) ÷ (+) = positive number

Examples

1. Find the product of –10 and 47.

2. What is the sum of –65 and –32?

3. Is the product of −7 and 4 less than −7, between −7 and 4, or greater than 4?

4. What is the value of −16 divided by 2.5?

ORDER OF OPERATIONS

Operations in a mathematical expression are always performed in a specific order, which is described by the acronym PEMDAS:

1. Parentheses
2. Exponents
3. Multiplication
4. Division
5. Addition
6. Subtraction

> ✔
> Can you come up with a mnemonic device to help yourself remember the order of operations?

Perform the operations within parentheses first, and then address any exponents. After those steps, perform all multiplication and division. These are carried out from left to right as they appear in the problem.

Finally, do all required addition and subtraction, also from left to right as each operation appears in the problem.

Examples

5. Solve: $-(2)^2 - (4 + 7)$

6. Solve: $(5)^2 \div 5 + 4 \times 2$

7. Solve the expression: $15 \times (4 + 8) - 3^3$

8. Solve the expression: $\left(\frac{5}{2} \times 4\right) + 23 - 4^2$

DECIMALS AND FRACTIONS

Numbers are written using the base-10 system where each digit (the numeric symbols 0 – 9) in a number is worth ten times as much as the number to the right of it. For example, in the number 37 each digit has a place value based on its location. The 3 is in the tens place, and so has a value of 30, and the 7 is in the ones place, so it has a value of 7.

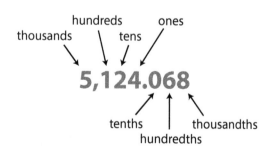

Figure 1.3. Place Value

Adding and Subtracting Decimals

When adding and subtracting decimals, write the numbers so that the decimal points are aligned. You want to subtract the ones place from the ones place, the tenths place from the tenths place, etc.

Examples

9. Find the sum of 17.07 and 2.52.

10. Jeannette has 7.4 gallons of gas in her tank. After driving, she has 6.8 gallons. How many gallons of gas did she use?

Multiplying and Dividing Decimals

When multiplying decimals, start by multiplying the numbers normally. You can then determine the placement of the decimal point in the result by adding the number of digits after the decimal in each of the numbers you multiplied together.

When dividing decimals, you should move the decimal point in the divisor (the number you're dividing by) until it is a whole number. You can then move the decimal in the dividend (the number you're dividing into) the same number of places in the same direction. Finally, divide the new numbers normally to get the correct answer.

Examples

11. What is the product of 0.25 and 1.3?

12. Find $0.8 \div 0.2$.

13. Find the quotient when 40 is divided by 0.25.

Working with Fractions

FRACTIONS are made up of two parts: the **NUMERATOR**, which appears above the bar, and the **DENOMINATOR**, which is below it. If a fraction is in its **SIMPLEST FORM**, the numerator and the denominator share no common factors. A fraction with a numerator larger than or equal to its denominator is an **IMPROPER FRACTION**; when the denominator is larger, it's a **PROPER FRACTION**.

Improper fractions can be converted into mixed numbers by dividing the numerator by the denominator. The resulting whole number is placed to the left of the fraction, and the remainder becomes the new numerator; the denominator does not change. The new number is called a **MIXED NUMBER** because it contains a whole number and a fraction. Mixed numbers can be turned into improper fractions through the reverse process: multiply the whole number by the denominator and add the numerator to get the new numerator.

Examples

14. Simplify the fraction $\frac{121}{77}$.

15. Convert $\frac{37}{5}$ into a mixed number.

Multiplying and Dividing Fractions

To multiply fractions, convert any mixed numbers into improper fractions and multiply the numerators together and the denominators together. Reduce to lowest terms if needed.

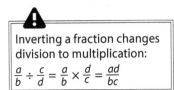

Inverting a fraction changes division to multiplication:
$$\frac{a}{b} \div \frac{c}{d} = \frac{a}{b} \times \frac{d}{c} = \frac{ad}{bc}$$

To divide fractions, first convert any mixed numbers into improper fractions. Then, invert the second fraction so that the denominator and numerator are switched. Finally, multiply the numerators together and the denominators together.

Examples

16. What is the product of $\frac{1}{12}$ and $\frac{6}{8}$?

17. Find $\frac{7}{8} \div \frac{1}{4}$.

18. $\frac{2}{5} \div 1\frac{1}{5} =$

19. A recipe calls for $\frac{1}{4}$ cup of sugar. If $8\frac{1}{2}$ batches of the recipe are needed, how many cups of sugar will be used?

Adding and Subtracting Fractions

Adding and subtracting fractions requires a **COMMON DENOMINATOR**. To get a common denominator, you can multiply each fraction by the number 1. With fractions, any number over itself (e.g., $\frac{5}{5}$, $\frac{12}{12}$, etc.) is equivalent to 1, so multiplying by such a fraction can change the denominator without changing the value of the fraction. Once the denominators are the same, the numerators can be added or subtracted.

The phrase *simplify the expression* just means you need to perform all the operations in the expression.

To add mixed numbers, you can first add the whole numbers and then the fractions. To subtract mixed numbers, convert each mixed number to an improper fraction, get a common denominator, and then subtract the numerators.

Examples

20. Simplify the expression $\frac{2}{3} - \frac{1}{5}$.

21. Find $2\frac{1}{3} - \frac{3}{2}$.

22. Find the sum of $\frac{9}{16}$, $\frac{1}{2}$, and $\frac{7}{4}$.

23. Sabrina has $\frac{2}{3}$ of a can of red paint. Her friend Amos has $\frac{1}{6}$ of a can. How much red paint do they have combined?

Converting Decimals to Fractions

To convert a decimal, simply use the numbers that come after the decimal as the numerator in the fraction. The denominator will be a power of 10 that matches the place value for the original decimal. For example, the denominator for 0.46 would be 100 because the last number is in the hundredths place; likewise, the denominator for 0.657 would be 1000 because the last number is in the thousandths place. Once this fraction has been set up, all that's left is to simplify it.

To convert a fraction to a decimal, just divide the numerator by the denominator on your calculator.

Example

24. Convert 0.45 into a fraction.

COMPARISON OF RATIONAL NUMBERS

Number comparison problems present numbers in different formats and ask which is larger or smaller, or whether the numbers are equivalent. The important step in solving these problems is to convert the numbers to the same format so that it is easier to see how they compare. If numbers are given in the same format, or after they have been converted, determine which number is smaller or if the numbers are equal. Remember that for negative numbers, higher numbers are actually smaller.

 To order numbers from least to greatest (or greatest to least), convert them to the same format and place them on a number line.

Examples

25. Which of the following values is the largest? 0.49, $\frac{3}{5}$, $\frac{1}{2}$, 0.55

26. Place the following numbers in order from least to greatest: $\frac{2}{5}$, −0.7, 0.35, $-\frac{3}{2}$, 0.46

RATIOS

A **RATIO** tells you how many of one thing exist in relation to the number of another thing. Unlike fractions, ratios do not give a part relative to a whole; instead, they compare two values. For example, if you have three apples and four oranges, the ratio of apples to oranges is 3 to 4. Ratios can be written using words (3 to 4), fractions $\left(\frac{3}{4}\right)$, or colons (3:4).

In order to work with ratios, it's helpful to rewrite them as a fraction expressing a part to a whole. For example, in the example above you have seven total pieces of fruit, so the fraction of your fruit that are apples is $\frac{3}{7}$, and oranges make up $\frac{4}{7}$ of your fruit collection.

One last important thing to consider when working with ratios is the units of the values being compared. On the Applied Math Assessment, you may be asked to rewrite a ratio using the same units on both sides. For example, you might have to rewrite the ratio 3 minutes to 7 seconds as 180 seconds to 7 seconds.

Examples

27. There are 90 voters in a room, and each is either a Democrat or a Republican. The ratio of Democrats to Republicans is 5:4. How many Republicans are there?

28. The ratio of students to teachers in a school is 15:1. If there are 38 teachers, how many students attend the school?

PROPORTIONS

A **PROPORTION** is an equation which states that two ratios are equal. Proportions are usually written as two fractions joined by an equal sign $\left(\frac{a}{b} = \frac{c}{d}\right)$, but they can also be written using colons ($a : b :: c : d$). Note that in a proportion, the units must be the same in both numerators and in both denominators.

Proportion problems on the Applied Math Assessment are usually word problems that include: distance and time, cost, or measurement.

Often you will be given three of the values in a proportion and asked to find the fourth. In these types of problems, you can solve for the missing variable by cross-multiplying—multiply the numerator of each fraction by the denominator of the other to get an equation with no fractions as shown below. You can then solve the equation using basic algebra.

$$\frac{a}{b} = \frac{c}{d} \rightarrow ad = bc$$

Examples

29. A train traveling 120 miles takes 3 hours to get to its destination. How long will it take for the train to travel 180 miles?

30. One acre of wheat requires 500 gallons of water. How many acres can be watered with 2600 gallons?

PERCENTAGES

A **PERCENT** is the ratio of a part to the whole multiplied by 100. The equation for percentages can be rearranged to solve for either the part, the whole, or the percent:

$$percent = \frac{part}{whole}$$

$$part = whole \times percent$$

$$whole = \frac{part}{percent}$$

In the equations above, the percent should always be expressed as a decimal. In order to convert a decimal into a percentage value, simply multiply it by 100. So, if you've read 5 pages (the part) of a 10-page article (the whole), you've read $\frac{5}{10} = 0.5 = 50\%$. (The percent sign (%) is used once the decimal has been multiplied by 100.)

Note that when solving these problems, the units for the part and the whole should be the same. If you're reading a book, saying you've read 5 pages out of 15 chapters doesn't make any sense.

The word *of* usually indicates what the whole is in a problem. For example, the problem might say *Ella ate two slices of the pizza*, which means the pizza is the whole.

Examples

31. 45 is 15% of what number?

32. Jim spent 30% of his paycheck at the fair. He spent $15 for a hat, $30 for a shirt, and $20 playing games. How much was his check? (Round to nearest dollar.)

33. What percent of 65 is 39?

34. Greta and Max sell cable subscriptions. In a given month, Greta sells 45 subscriptions and Max sells 51. If 240 total subscriptions were sold in that month, what percent were not sold by Greta or Max?

35. Grant needs to score 75% on an exam. If the exam has 45 questions, how many questions does he need to answer correctly?

PERCENT CHANGE

PERCENT CHANGE problems will ask you to calculate how much a given quantity changed. The problems are solved in a similar way to regular percent problems, except that instead of using the *part* you'll use the *amount of change*. Note that the sign of the *amount of change* is important: if the original amount has increased the change will be positive, and if it has decreased the change will be negative. Again, in the equations below the percent is a decimal value; you need to multiply by 100 to get the actual percentage.

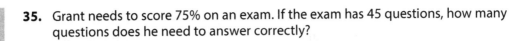

Words that indicate a percent change problem: *discount, markup, sale, increase, decrease*

$$percent\ change = \frac{amount\ of\ change}{original\ amount}$$

$$amount\ of\ change = original\ amount \times percent\ change$$

$$original\ amount = \frac{amount\ of\ change}{percent\ change}$$

Examples

36. A computer software retailer marks up its games by 40% above the wholesale price when it sells them to customers. Find the price of a game for a customer if the game costs the retailer $25.

37. A golf shop pays its wholesaler $40 for a certain club, and then sells it to a golfer for $75. What is the markup rate?

38. A store charges a 40% markup on the shoes it sells. How much did the store pay for a pair of shoes purchased by a customer for $63?

39. An item originally priced at $55 is marked 25% off. What is the sale price?

UNITS OF MEASUREMENT

The ACT WorkKeys® Applied Math Assessment will test your knowledge of two types of units: the US customary (or American) system and the metric system. The US system includes many of the units you likely use in day-to-day activities, such as the foot, pound, and cup. The metric system is used throughout the rest of the world and is the main system used in science and medicine. Common units for the US and metric systems are shown in the table below.

Table 1.1. Units

DIMENSION	US CUSTOMARY	METRIC
length	inch/foot/yard/mile	meter
mass	ounce/pound/ton	gram
volume	cup/pint/quart/gallon	liter
temperature	Fahrenheit	Celsius or kelvin

The metric system uses prefixes to simplify large and small numbers. These prefixes are added to the base units shown in the table above. For example, the measurement 1000 meters can be written using the prefix kilo– as 1 kilometer. The most commonly used metric prefixes are given in the table below.

Table 1.2. Metric Prefixes

PREFIX	SYMBOL	MULTIPLICATION FACTOR
kilo	k	1,000
hecto	h	100
deca	da	10
base unit	--	--
deci	d	0.1
centi	c	0.01
milli	m	0.001

Conversion factors can be used to convert between units both within a single system and between the US and metric systems. Some questions on the Applied Math Assessment will require you to know common conversion factors, some of which are shown in the table below.

Table 1.3. Conversion Factors

1 in = 2.54 cm	1 lb = 0.454 kg
1 yd = 0.914 m	1 cal = 4.19 J
1 mi = 1.61 km	$C = \frac{5}{9}(^{\circ}F - 32)$
1 gal = 3.785 L	1 cm³ = 1 mL
1 oz = 28.35 g	1 hr = 3600 s

To perform unit conversion, start with the initial value and multiply by a conversion factor to reach the final unit. This process is shown in Figure 1.4.

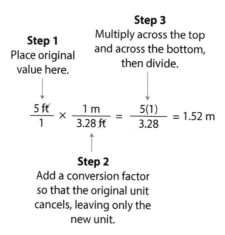

Figure 1.4. Unit Conversion

Examples

40. Convert 4.25 km to meters.

41. What is the mass in kilograms of a 150 lb man?

42. A ball rolling across a table travels 6 inches per second. How many feet will it travel in 1 minute?

AREA AND PERIMETER

Most of the geometry problems on the ACT WorkKeys® will require you to find either the area inside a shape or its perimeter (the distance around it). The perimeter is found by simply adding the lengths of all the sides. (Perimeter uses units for *length*, such as feet, inches, or meters. Because area is found by multiplying two lengths, it has units of *length squared*, such as square feet, ft², or square meters, m².) You will receive a formula sheet on the exam for the area of basic shapes, including triangles, rectangles, and circles. Still, it's a good idea to have some of these formulas committed to memory.

Table 1.4. Area and Perimeter of Basic Shapes

SHAPE	EXAMPLE	AREA	PERIMETER
Triangle	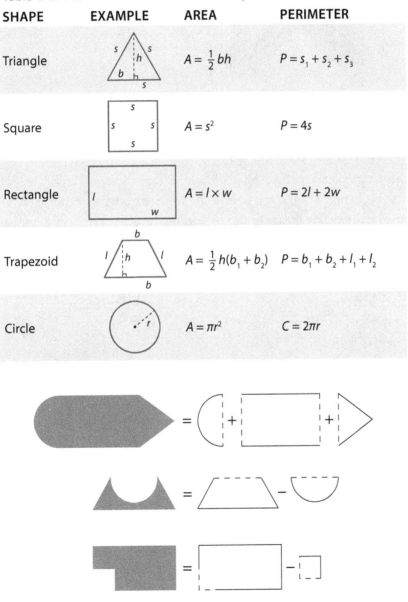	$A = \frac{1}{2}bh$	$P = s_1 + s_2 + s_3$
Square		$A = s^2$	$P = 4s$
Rectangle		$A = l \times w$	$P = 2l + 2w$
Trapezoid		$A = \frac{1}{2}h(b_1 + b_2)$	$P = b_1 + b_2 + l_1 + l_2$
Circle		$A = \pi r^2$	$C = 2\pi r$

Figure 1.5. Compound Shapes

Some questions on the Applied Math Assessment, generally around level 6 or 7, will include area and perimeter problems with compound shapes. These are complex shapes made by combining more basic shapes. While they might look complicated, they can be solved by simply breaking the compound shape apart and using the formulas given above.

Examples

43. A farmer has purchased 100 m of fencing to put around his rectangular garden. If one side of the garden is 20 m long and the other is 28 m, how much fencing will the farmer have left over?

44. What is the area of the shaded region?

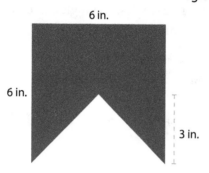

THREE-DIMENSIONAL SHAPES

You may also see problems on the Applied Math Assessment that include three-dimensional shapes. These problems will ask you to find the volume of the shape or its surface area (the area of all its sides). Surface area is found by adding the area of each face on the shape. The formulas for the volume of common three-dimensional shapes are given in the table below.

Table 1.5. Volume of Basic Solids

SOLID	VOLUME
sphere (r is radius)	$V = \frac{4}{3}\pi r^3$
cube (s is side)	$V = s^3$
cylinder (r is radius of base; h is height)	$V = \pi r^2 h$
right rectangular prism (h is height; B is area of base)	$V = Bh$

Examples

45. What is the surface area of a cube with a side length of 5 mm?

46. What is the volume of a sphere with a radius of 3 cm?

GRAPHS AND CHARTS

Most questions with visual aids like graphs and charts appear on the Graphic Literacy Assessment (see chapter 2). However, you may see some questions on the Applied Math Assessment that use these visual tools. These questions require you to interpret information from graphs and charts; they will be pretty straightforward as long as you pay careful attention to detail. There are several different graph and chart types that may appear on the Applied Math Assessment of the ACT WorkKeys®.

Bar Graphs and Histograms

BAR GRAPHS present the numbers of an item that exist in different categories. The categories are shown on one axis, and the number of items is shown on the other axis. Bar graphs are usually used to easily compare amounts.

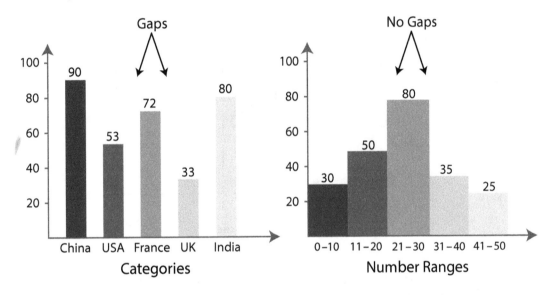

Bar Graph　　　　**Histogram**

Figure 1.6. Bar Graph versus Histogram

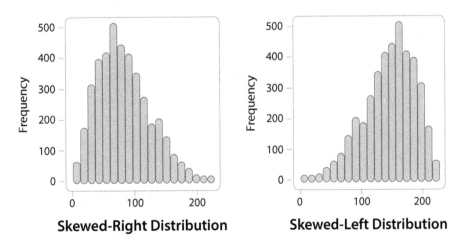

Skewed-Right Distribution　　**Skewed-Left Distribution**

Figure 1.7. Histogram Skew

Histograms similarly use bars to compare data, but the independent variable is a continuous variable that has been "binned" or divided into categories. For example, the time of day can be broken down into 8:00 a.m. to 12:00 p.m., 12:00 p.m. to 4:00 p.m., and so on. Usually (but not always), a gap is included between the bars of a bar graph but not a histogram.

Histograms can be symmetrical, skewed left or right, or multimodal (data spread around). Note that SKEWED LEFT means the peak of the data is on the *right*, with a tail to the left, while SKEWED RIGHT means the peak is on the *left*, with a tail to the right. This seems counterintuitive to many; the "left" or "right" always refers to the tail of the data. This is because a long tail to the right, for example, means there are high outlier values that are skewing the data to the right.

Examples

47. The graph below shows rainfall in inches per month. Which month had the least amount of rainfall? Which had the most?

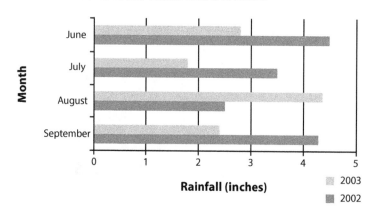

48. According to the graph below, how many more ice cream cones were sold in July than in September?

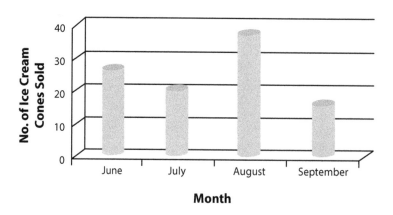

Pie Charts

PIE CHARTS present parts of a whole and are often used with percentages. Together, all the slices of the pie add up to the total number of items, or 100%.

Examples

Use the pie chart below for questions 49 and 50.

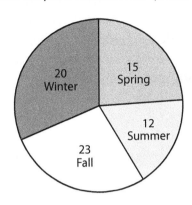

49. The pie chart shows the distribution of birthdays in a class of students. How many students have birthdays in the spring or summer?

50. What percentage of students have birthdays in winter? Round to the nearest tenth of a percent.

Line Graphs

LINE GRAPHS show trends over time. The number of each item represented by the graph will be on the *y*-axis, and time will be on the *x*-axis.

Examples

Use the line graph below for questions 51 and 52.

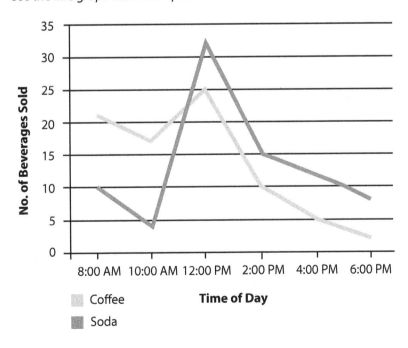

51. The line graph shows beverage sales at an airport snack shop throughout the day. Which beverage sold more at 4:00 p.m.?

52. At what time of day were the most beverages sold?

MEASURES OF CENTRAL TENDENCY

MEAN is a math term for average. To find the mean, total all the terms and divide by the number of terms. The **MEDIAN** is the middle number of a given set. To find the median, put the terms in numerical order; the middle number will be the median. In the case of a set of even numbers, the middle two numbers are averaged. **MODE** is the number which occurs most frequently within a given set.

It is possible to have more than one mode.

Examples

53. Find the mean of 24, 27, and 18.

54. The mean of three numbers is 45. If two of the numbers are 38 and 43, what is the third number?

55. What is the median of 24, 27, and 18?

56. What is the median of 24, 27, 18, and 19?

57. What is the mode of 2, 5, 4, 4, 3, 2, 8, 9, 2, 7, 2, and 2?

ANSWER KEY

1. Find the product of −10 and 47.

   $(-) \times (+) = (-)$

   $-10 \times 47 = \textbf{−470}$

2. What is the sum of −65 and −32?

   $(-) + (-) = (-)$

   $-65 + -32 = \textbf{−97}$

3. Is the product of −7 and 4 less than −7, between −7 and 4, or greater than 4?

   $(-) \times (+) = (-)$

   $-7 \times 4 = -28$, which is **less than −7**

4. What is the value of −16 divided by 2.5?

   $(-) \div (+) = (-)$

   $-16 \div 2.5 = \textbf{−6.4}$

5. Solve: $-(2)^2 - (4 + 7)$

   First, complete operations within parentheses:

   $-(2)^2 - (11)$

   Second, calculate the value of exponential expressions:

   $-(4) - (11)$

   Finally, do addition and subtraction:

   $-4 - 11 = \textbf{−15}$

6. Solve: $(5)^2 \div 5 + 4 \times 2$

   First, calculate the value of exponential expressions:

   $(25) \div 5 + 4 \times 2$

   Second, calculate division and multiplication from left to right: $5 + 8$

   Finally, do addition and subtraction: $5 + 8 = \textbf{13}$

7. Solve the expression: $15 \times (4 + 8) - 3^3$

   First, complete operations within parentheses:

   $15 \times (12) - 3^3$

   Second, calculate the value of exponential expressions:

   $15 \times (12) - 27$

   Third, calculate division and multiplication from left to right:

   $180 - 27$

   Finally, do addition and subtraction from left to right:

   $180 - 27 = \textbf{153}$

8. Solve the expression:

   $\left(\frac{5}{2} \times 4\right) + 23 - 4^2$

   First, complete operations within parentheses:

   $(10) + 23 - 4^2$

   Second, calculate the value of exponential expressions:

   $(10) + 23 - 16$

   Finally, do addition and subtraction from left to right:

   $10 + 23 - 16$

   $33 - 16 = \textbf{17}$

9. Find the sum of 17.07 and 2.52.

   $\begin{array}{r} 17.07 \\ +\ \ 2.52 \\ \hline = 19.59 \end{array}$

   = **19.59**

10. Jeannette has 7.4 gallons of gas in her tank. After driving, she has 6.8 gallons. How many gallons of gas did she use?

    $\begin{array}{r} 7.4 \\ -\ 6.8 \\ \hline = 0.6 \end{array}$

    = **0.6 gal.**

11. What is the product of 0.25 and 1.3?

    $25 \times 13 = 325$

    There are two digits after the decimal in 0.25 and one digit after the decimal in 1.3. Therefore the product should have three digits after the decimal: **0.325**.

12. Find $0.8 \div 0.2$.

    Change 0.2 to 2 by moving the decimal one space to the right.

Next, move the decimal one space to the right on the dividend. 0.8 becomes 8.

Now, divide 8 by 2. $8 \div 2 = \mathbf{4}$

13. Find the quotient when 40 is divided by 0.25.

First, change the divisor to a whole number: 0.25 becomes 25.

Next, change the dividend to match the divisor by moving the decimal two spaces to the right, so 40 becomes 4000.

Now divide: $4000 \div 25 = \mathbf{160}$

14. Simplify the fraction $\frac{121}{77}$.

121 and 77 share a common factor of 11. So, if we divide each by 11 we can simplify the fraction:

$$\frac{121}{77} = \frac{11}{11} \times \frac{11}{7} = \mathbf{\frac{11}{7}}$$

15. Convert $\frac{37}{5}$ into a mixed number.

Start by dividing the numerator by the denominator:

$37 \div 5 = 7$ with a remainder of 2

Now build a mixed number with the whole number and the new numerator:

$$\frac{37}{5} = \mathbf{7\frac{2}{5}}$$

16. What is the product of $\frac{1}{12}$ and $\frac{6}{8}$?

Simply multiply the numerators together and the denominators together, then reduce:

$$\frac{1}{12} \times \frac{6}{8} = \frac{6}{96} = \mathbf{\frac{1}{16}}$$

Sometimes it's easier to reduce fractions before multiplying if you can:

$$\frac{1}{12} \times \frac{6}{8} = \frac{1}{12} \times \frac{3}{4} = \frac{3}{48} = \mathbf{\frac{1}{16}}$$

17. Find $\frac{7}{8} \div \frac{1}{4}$.

For a fraction division problem, invert the second fraction and then multiply and reduce:

$$\frac{7}{8} \div \frac{1}{4} = \frac{7}{8} \times \frac{4}{1} = \frac{28}{8} = \mathbf{\frac{7}{2}}$$

18. $\frac{2}{5} \div 1\frac{1}{5} =$

This is a fraction division problem, so the first step is to convert the mixed number to an improper fraction:

$$1\frac{1}{5} = \frac{5 \times 1}{5} + \frac{1}{5} = \frac{6}{5}$$

Now, divide the fractions. Remember to invert the second fraction, and then multiply normally:

$$\frac{2}{5} \div \frac{6}{5} = \frac{2}{5} \times \frac{5}{6} = \frac{10}{30} = \mathbf{\frac{1}{3}}$$

19. A recipe calls for $\frac{1}{4}$ cup of sugar. If $8\frac{1}{2}$ batches of the recipe are needed, how many cups of sugar will be used?

This is a fraction multiplication problem: $\frac{1}{4} \times 8\frac{1}{2}$.

First, we need to convert the mixed number into a proper fraction:

$$8\frac{1}{2} = \frac{8 \times 2}{2} + \frac{1}{2} = \frac{17}{2}$$

Now, multiply the fractions across the numerators and denominators, and then reduce:

$$\frac{1}{4} \times 8\frac{1}{2} = \frac{1}{4} \times \frac{17}{2} = \mathbf{\frac{17}{8}} \text{ cups of sugar, or } \mathbf{2\frac{1}{8}}$$

20. Simplify the expression $\frac{2}{3} - \frac{1}{5}$.

First, multiply each fraction by a factor of 1 to get a common denominator. How do you know which factor of 1 to use? Look at the other fraction and use the number found in that denominator:

$$\frac{2}{3} - \frac{1}{5} = \frac{2}{3}\left(\frac{5}{5}\right) - \frac{1}{5}\left(\frac{3}{3}\right) = \frac{10}{15} - \frac{3}{15}$$

Once the fractions have a common denominator, simply subtract the numerators:

$$\frac{10}{15} - \frac{3}{15} = \mathbf{\frac{7}{15}}$$

21. Find $2\frac{1}{3} - \frac{3}{2}$.

This is a fraction subtraction problem with a mixed number, so the first step is to convert the mixed number to an improper fraction:

$$2\frac{1}{3} = \frac{2 \times 3}{3} + \frac{1}{3} = \frac{7}{3}$$

Next, convert each fraction so they share a common denominator:

$$\frac{7}{3} \times \frac{2}{2} = \frac{14}{6}$$

$$\frac{3}{2} \times \frac{3}{3} = \frac{9}{6}$$

Now, subtract the fractions by subtracting the numerators:

$$\frac{14}{6} - \frac{9}{6} = \frac{5}{6}$$

22. Find the sum of $\frac{9}{16}, \frac{1}{2},$ and $\frac{7}{4}$.

For this fraction addition problem, we need to find a common denominator. Notice that 2 and 4 are both factors of 16, so 16 can be the common denominator:

$$\frac{1}{2} \times \frac{8}{8} = \frac{8}{16}$$
$$\frac{7}{4} \times \frac{4}{4} = \frac{28}{16}$$
$$\frac{9}{16} + \frac{8}{16} + \frac{28}{16} = \frac{45}{16}$$

23. Sabrina has $\frac{2}{3}$ of a can of red paint. Her friend Amos has $\frac{1}{6}$ of a can. How much red paint do they have combined?

To add fractions, make sure that they have a common denominator. Since 3 is a factor of 6, 6 can be the common denominator:

$$\frac{2}{3} \times \frac{2}{2} = \frac{4}{6}$$

Now, add the numerators:

$$\frac{4}{6} + \frac{1}{6} = \frac{5}{6} \textbf{ of a can}$$

24. Convert 0.45 into a fraction.

The last number in the decimal is in the hundredths place, so we can easily set up a fraction:

$$0.45 = \frac{45}{100}$$

The next step is to simply reduce the fraction down to the lowest common denominator. Here, both 45 and 100 are divisible by 5:

$$\frac{45}{100} = \frac{(45 \div 5)}{(100 \div 5)} = \frac{9}{20}$$

25. Which of the following values is the largest? $0.49, \frac{3}{5}, \frac{1}{2}, 0.55$

Convert the fractions to decimals:

$$\frac{3}{5} = 0.6$$
$$\frac{1}{2} = 0.5$$

Place the values in order from smallest to largest:

$$0.49 < 0.5 < 0.55 < 0.6$$

$\frac{3}{5}$ **is the largest number.**

26. Place the following numbers in order from least to greatest:
$\frac{2}{5}, -0.7, 0.35, -\frac{3}{2}, 0.46$

Convert the fractions to decimals:

$$\frac{2}{5} = 0.4$$
$$-\frac{3}{2} = -1.5$$

Place the values in order from smallest to largest:

$$-1.5 < -0.7 < 0.35 < 0.4 < 0.46$$

Put the numbers back in their original form:

$$-\frac{3}{2} < -0.7 < 0.35 < \frac{2}{5} < 0.46$$

27. There are 90 voters in a room, and each is either a Democrat or a Republican. The ratio of Democrats to Republicans is 5:4. How many Republicans are there?

We know that there are 5 Democrats for every 4 Republicans in the room, which means for every 9 people, 4 are Republicans.

$$5 + 4 = 9$$

Fraction of Republicans: $\frac{4}{9}$

If $\frac{4}{9}$ of the 90 voters are Republicans, then:

$$\frac{4}{9} \times 90 = \textbf{40 voters are Republicans}$$

28. The ratio of students to teachers in a school is 15:1. If there are 38 teachers, how many students attend the school?

To solve this ratio problem, we can simply multiply both sides of the ratio by the desired value to find the number of students that correspond to having 38 teachers:

$$\frac{15 \text{ students}}{1 \text{ teacher}} \times 38 \text{ teachers} = 570 \text{ students}$$

The school has **570 students.**

29. A train traveling 120 miles takes 3 hours to get to its destination. How long will it take for the train to travel 180 miles?

Start by setting up the proportion:

$$\frac{120 \text{ miles}}{3 \text{ hours}} = \frac{180 \text{ miles}}{x \text{ hours}}$$

Note that it doesn't matter which value is placed in the numerator or denominator, as long as it is the same on both sides. Now, solve for the missing quantity through cross-multiplication:

120 miles × x hours = 3 hours × 180 miles

Now solve the equation:

$$x \text{ hours} = \frac{(3 \text{ hours}) \times (180 \text{ miles})}{120 \text{ miles}}$$

x = 4.5 hours

30. One acre of wheat requires 500 gallons of water. How many acres can be watered with 2600 gallons?

Set up the equation:

$$\frac{1 \text{ acre}}{500 \text{ gal.}} = \frac{x \text{ acres}}{2600 \text{ gal.}}$$

Then solve for x:

$$x \text{ acres} = \frac{1 \text{ acre} \times 2600 \text{ gal}}{500 \text{ gal}}$$

$$x = \frac{26}{5} \text{ or } \textbf{5.2 acres}$$

31. 45 is 15% of what number?

Set up the appropriate equation and solve. Don't forget to change 15% to a decimal value:

$$whole = \frac{part}{percent} = \frac{45}{0.15} = \textbf{300}$$

32. Jim spent 30% of his paycheck at the fair. He spent $15 for a hat, $30 for a shirt, and $20 playing games. How much was his check? (Round to nearest dollar.)

Set up the appropriate equation and solve:

$$whole = \frac{part}{percent} = \frac{15 + 30 + 20}{0.30} = \textbf{\$217.00}$$

33. What percent of 65 is 39?

Set up the equation and solve:

$$percent = \frac{part}{whole} = \frac{39}{65} = \textbf{0.6 or 60\%}$$

34. Greta and Max sell cable subscriptions. In a given month, Greta sells 45 subscriptions and Max sells 51. If 240 total subscriptions were sold in that month, what percent were not sold by Greta or Max?

You can use the information in the question to figure out what percentage of subscriptions were sold by Max and Greta:

$$percent = \frac{part}{whole} = \frac{(51 + 45)}{240} = \frac{96}{240} = 0.4$$

or 40%

However, the question asks how many subscriptions weren't sold by Max or Greta. If they sold 40%, then the other salespeople sold 100% − 40% = **60%**.

35. Grant needs to score 75% on an exam. If the exam has 45 questions, how many questions does he need to answer correctly?

Set up the equation and solve. Remember to convert 75% to a decimal value:

$part = whole \times percent = 45 \times 0.75 =$ 33.75, so he needs to answer at least **34 questions correctly**.

36. A computer software retailer marks up its games by 40% above the wholesale price when it sells them to customers. Find the price of a game for a customer if the game costs the retailer $25.

Set up the appropriate equation and solve:

$amount\ of\ change = original\ amount \times percent\ change = 25 \times 0.4 = 10$

If the amount of change is 10, that means the store adds a markup of $10, so the game costs:

$25 + $10 = **$35**

37. A golf shop pays its wholesaler $40 for a certain club, and then sells it to a golfer for $75. What is the markup rate?

First, calculate the amount of change:

$75 − 40 = 35$

Now you can set up the equation and solve. (Note that *markup rate* is another way of saying *percent change*):

$$percent\ change = \frac{amount\ of\ change}{original\ amount} = \frac{35}{40}$$

$= 0.875 = \textbf{87.5\%}$

38. A store charges a 40% markup on the shoes it sells. How much did the store pay for a pair of shoes purchased by a customer for $63?

You're solving for the original price, but it's going to be tricky because you don't know the amount of change; you only know the new price. To solve, you need to create an expression for the amount of change:

If *original amount* = *x*

Then *amount of change* = 63 − *x*

Now you can plug these values into your equation:

original amount = $\frac{amount\ of\ change}{percent\ change}$

$x = \frac{63 - x}{0.4}$

The last step is to solve for *x*:

$0.4x = 63 - x$

$1.4x = 63$

$x = 45$

The store paid **$45 for the shoes**.

39. An item originally priced at $55 is marked 25% off. What is the sale price?

You've been asked to find the sale price, which means you need to solve for the amount of change first:

amount of change = *original amount* × *percent change* =

$55 \times 0.25 = 13.75$

Using this amount, you can find the new price. Because it's on sale, we know the item will cost less than the original price:

$55 - 13.75 = 41.25$

The sale price is $41.25.

40. Convert 4.25 km to meters.

$\frac{4.25\ km}{1} \times \frac{1000\ m}{1\ km} = \textbf{4250 m}$

41. What is the mass in kilograms of a 150 lb man?

$\frac{150\ lb}{1} \times \frac{0.454\ kg}{1\ lb} = (150)(0.454) = \textbf{68.1 kg}$

42. A ball rolling across a table travels 6 inches per second. How many feet will it travel in 1 minute?

This problem requires two unit conversions. Start by converting inches to feet:

$\frac{6\ in}{1\ s} \times \frac{1\ ft}{12\ in} = \frac{0.5\ ft}{1\ s}$

Now convert seconds to minutes:

$\frac{0.5\ ft}{1\ s} \times \frac{60\ s}{1\ min} = \frac{30\ ft}{1\ min}$

The ball will travel **30 feet** in 1 minute.

43. A farmer has purchased 100 m of fencing to put around his rectangular garden. If one side of the garden is 20 m long and the other is 28 m, how much fencing will the farmer have left over?

The perimeter of a rectangle is equal to twice its length plus twice its width:

$P = 2(20) + 2(28) = 96$ m

The farmer has 100 m of fencing, so subtract to find the amount of fence left:

$100 - 96 = \textbf{4 m}$

44. What is the area of the shaded region?

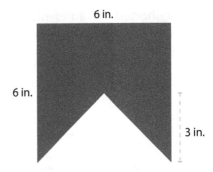

6 in.

6 in.

3 in.

The figure is a square with a triangle cut out. First, find the area of the square:

$A = s^2 = 6^2 = 36$ in²

Now find the area of the triangle:

$A = \frac{1}{2}bh = \frac{1}{2}(6)(3) = 9$ in²

Subtract the area of the triangle from the area of the square:

$36 - 9 = \textbf{27 in}^2$

45. What is the surface area of a cube with a side length of 5 mm?

A cube has six faces, each of which is a square:

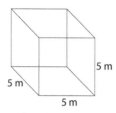

Find the area of each side using the formula for the area of a square:

$A = s^2 = 5^2 = 25$ m^2

Multiply the area by 6 (because the cube has six faces):

$SA = 25(6) = 150$ m^2

46. What is the volume of a sphere with a radius of 3 cm?

Use the formula for the volume of a sphere:

$V = \frac{4}{3}\pi r^3 = \frac{4}{3}\pi(3)^3 = $ **36π cm^3**

47. The graph below shows rainfall in inches per month. Which month had the least amount of rainfall? Which had the most?

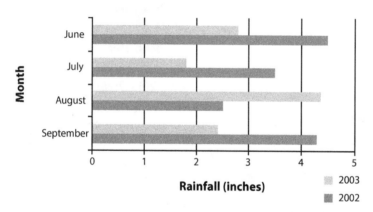

The shortest bar represents the month with the least rain, and the longest bar represents the month with the most rain: **July 2003 had the least**, and **June 2002 had the most**.

48. According to the graph below, how many more ice cream cones were sold in July than in September?

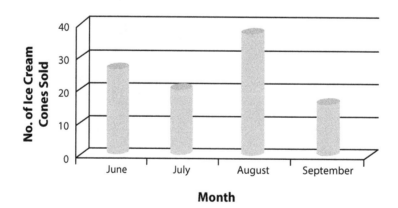

Tracing from the top of each bar to the scale on the left shows that sales in July were 20 and September sales were 15. So, **5 more cones were sold in July**.

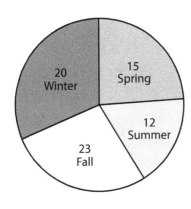

49. The pie chart shows the distribution of birthdays in a class of students. How many students have birthdays in the spring or summer?

   Fifteen students have birthdays in spring and 12 in summer, so there are **27 students** with birthdays in spring or summer.

50. What percentage of students have birthdays in winter? Round to the nearest tenth of a percent.

   Use the equation for percent:
   $$percent = \frac{part}{whole} = \frac{winter\ birthdays}{total\ birthdays} = \frac{20}{20 + 15 + 23 + 12} = \frac{20}{70} = \frac{2}{7} = 0.286\ or$$
   28.6%

51. The line graph shows beverage sales at an airport snack shop throughout the day. Which beverage sold more at 4:00 p.m.?

   At 4:00 p.m., approximately 12 sodas and 5 coffees were sold, so more **soda** was sold.

52. At what time of day were the most beverages sold?

   This question is asking for the time of day with the most sales of coffee and soda combined. It is not necessary to add up sales at each time of day to find the answer. Just from looking at the graph, you can see that sales for both beverages were highest at noon, so the answer must be **12:00 p.m**.

53. Find the mean of 24, 27, and 18.

   Add the terms, then divide by the number of terms:
   $$mean = \frac{24 + 27 + 18}{3} = 23$$

54. The mean of three numbers is 45. If two of the numbers are 38 and 43, what is the third number?

   Set up the equation for mean with x representing the third number, then solve:
   $$mean = \frac{38 + 43 + x}{3} = 45$$
   $$38 + 43 + x = 135$$
   $$x = 54$$

55. What is the median of 24, 27, and 18?

   Place the terms in order, then pick the middle term:

   18, 24, 27

   The median is **24**.

56. What is the median of 24, 27, 18, and 19?

   Place the terms in order. Because there are an even number of terms, the median will be the average of the middle 2 terms:

   18, 19, 24, 27
   $$median = \frac{19 + 24}{2} = 21.5$$

57. What is the mode of 2, 5, 4, 4, 3, 2, 8, 9, 2, 7, and 2?

   The mode is 2 because it appears the most within the set.

2

GRAPHIC LITERACY

The Graphic Literacy Assessment of the ACT WorkKeys® tests your comprehension of informational sources other than text passages. These questions will include visual information sources (maps, graphs, diagrams), text features (book indexes, tables of contents), printed communications (flyers, memos), or lists of instructions.

GRAPHS

Graphs are used to present numerical data in a way that is easy for the reader to understand. There are a number of different types of graphs, each of which is useful for different types of data.

BAR GRAPHS use bars of different lengths to compare amounts. The independent variable on a bar graph is grouped into categories such as months, flavors, or locations, and the dependent variable will be a quantity. Thus, comparing the lengths of the bars provides a visual guide to the relative quantities in each category.

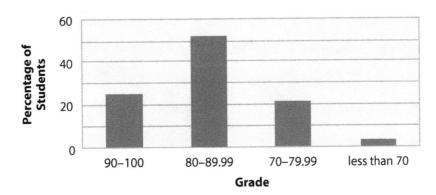

Figure 2.1. Bar Graph

SCATTERPLOTS use points to show relationships between two variables that can be plotted as coordinate points. One variable describes a position on the *x*-axis, and the other a point on the *y*-axis. Scatterplots can suggest relationships between variables. For example, both variables might increase, or one might increase when the other decreases.

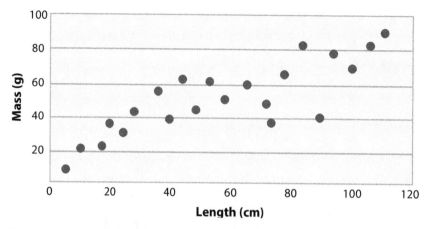

Figure 2.2. Scatterplot

LINE GRAPHS show changes in data by connecting points on a scatterplot using a line. These graphs will often measure time on the *x*-axis and are used to show trends in the data, such as temperature changes over a day or school attendance throughout the year.

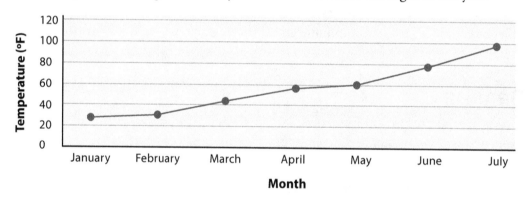

Figure 2.3. Line Graph

CIRCLE GRAPHS (also called pie charts) are used to show parts of a whole: the "pie" is the whole, and each "slice" represents a percentage or part of the whole.

Test Scores

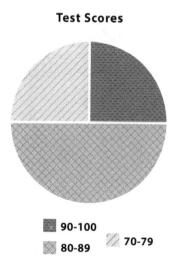

■ 90-100
■ 80-89   ▨ 70-79

Figure 2.4. Circle Graph

Examples

Use the pie chart below for questions 1 and 2.

Sales at Wholesale Electronics

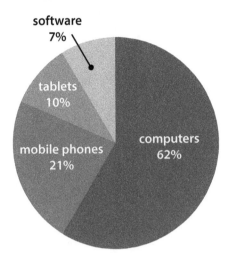

1. Which of the following products accounts for the largest share of Wholesale Electronics' total sales?

   A) mobile phones

   B) computers

   C) software and tablets

   D) software and mobile phones

2. Mobile phones and tablets make up what percentage of Wholesale Electronics' total sales?

   A) 17 percent

   B) 28 percent

   C) 31 percent

   D) 83 percent

MAPS

The **LEGEND** or **KEY** of a map explains the various symbols used on the map and their meanings and measurements. These symbols typically include a compass rose and a distance scale. A **COMPASS ROSE** indicates the four cardinal directions (north, south, west, and east) and the four intermediate directions (northwest, northeast, southwest, and southeast). A **DISTANCE SCALE** is used to show the ratio of the distance on the page to the actual distance between objects, usually in miles or kilometers.

Examples

Use the map below to answer questions 3 and 4.

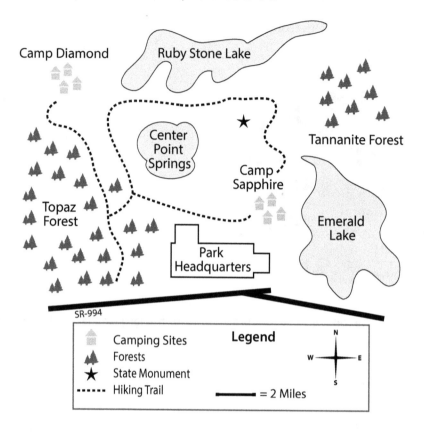

3. Which direction is Ruby Stone Lake from Park Headquarters?

   A) south

   B) northwest

   C) southwest

   D) north

4. Approximately how many miles is it from the state monument to the center of Tananite Forest?

   A) 1 mile

   B) 2 miles

   C) 4 miles

   D) 5 miles

SCALE READINGS

A scale reading is a numerical value collected from a scale or measurement device. On the ACT WorkKeys® Graphic Literacy Assessment, you may see devices like thermometers, blood pressure cuffs, or weight scales. To prepare for the exam, familiarize yourself with the standard units and displays for these devices.

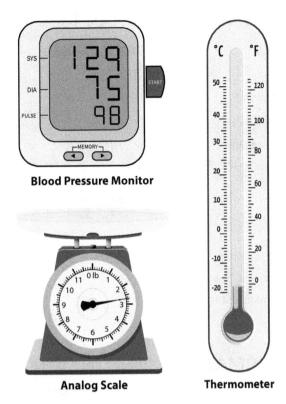

Blood Pressure Monitor

Analog Scale

Thermometer

Figure 2.5. Scale Readings

Examples

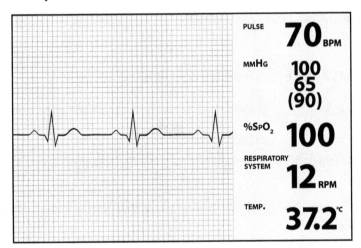

5. The figure shows the readout for a patient's EKG monitor. What is the patient's oxygen saturation?

A) 70 BPM

B) 100 mmHg

C) 100 percent

D) 37.2°C

6. The table below describes the categories for systolic blood pressure.

CATEGORIES	SYSTOLIC RANGE
Normal	< 120
Prehypertension	120 - 139
Hypertension Stage 1	140 - 159
Hypertension Stage 2	160 - 179
Hypertensive Crisis	> 180

The EKG monitor shows a patient who belongs in which of the following categories?

A) Normal
B) Prehypertension
C) Hypertension Stage 1
D) Hypertension Stage 2

PRODUCT INFORMATION

Product information questions ask you to use given information about products, such as price, shipping, or taxes, to compare the true cost of those products. (You may be required to perform basic arithmetic for some of the problems in this section.)

Examples

Use the table below to answer questions 7 and 8.

Shoe Prices

RETAILER	BASE PRICE	SHIPPING & HANDLING	TAXES
Wholesale Footwear	$59.99	$10.95	$7.68
Bargain Sales	$65.99	$5.95	$5.38
Famous Shoes	$79.99	$0.00	$4.89

7. Rachel wants to buy shoes and can't spend more than $80. Which retailer(s) can she shop at?

A) Wholesale Footwear and Bargain Sales
B) Famous Shoes
C) Wholesale Footwear and Famous Shoes
D) Bargain Sales and Famous Shoes

8. Allen has budgeted $6 for taxes and $6 for shipping and handling. Which retailer(s) can he shop at?

A) Bargain Sales and Famous Shoes
B) Wholesale Footwear and Famous Shoes
C) Wholesale Footwear
D) Bargain Sales and Wholesale Footwear

SETS OF DIRECTIONS

Some questions on the Graphic Literacy Assessment will require you to follow a set of simple directions. These directions can be given in a paragraph format or list format. Usually, each step, or direction, includes specific instructions that must be remembered in order to complete the subsequent steps. The directions will require you to manipulate quantities (such as money or numbers of items) or shapes to reach the final answer.

Write out the new answer for each step as you finish it so you can easily check your work.

Examples

9. You start with 3 red apples and 1 green apple in a basket. After following the directions below, how many apples are in the basket?

1. Remove 1 red apple.
2. Add 1 green apple.
3. Add 1 red apple.
4. Add 1 green apple.
5. Remove 2 red apples.
6. Remove 1 green apple.
7. Add 3 red apples.
8. Add 2 green apples.

A) 4 red apples and 2 green apples
B) 4 red apples and 4 green apples
C) 2 red apples and 3 green apples
D) 0 red apples and 3 green apples

10. You have 12 gallons of fuel in your tank. After following the directions below, how many gallons of fuel are left in the tank?

1. Use 1 gallon to drive to work.
2. Use 1 gallon to drive home.
3. Use 0.5 gallons to drive the kids to soccer practice.
4. Use 0.5 gallons to drive to the grocery store.
5. Use 2 gallons to drive back home.

A) 2 gallons
B) 5.5 gallons
C) 7 gallons
D) 8.5 gallons

INDEXES AND TABLES OF CONTENTS

An **INDEX** is an alphabetical list of topics, and their associated page numbers, covered in a text. A **TABLE OF CONTENTS** is an outline of a text that includes topics, organized by page number. Both of these can be used to look up information, but they have slightly different purposes. An index helps the reader determine where in the text he or she can find specific details. A table of contents shows the reader the general arrangement of the text.

When would it be appropriate to use an index but NOT a table of contents?

Examples

11. According to the index below, where might the reader find information about the nursing code of ethics?

A) pages 237 – 291

B) pages 189 – 296

C) pages 292 – 296

D) pages 189 – 236

12. A student has been assigned a set of homework questions from page 125. What topic will the questions cover?

TABLE OF CONTENTS

A) Pre-Algebra

B) Algebra

C) Geometry

D) Calculus

TEXT FEATURES

TEXT FEATURES are stylistic elements used to clarify, add meaning, or differentiate. Examples of text features include bold, italicized, or underlined fonts, and bulleted or numbered lists.

Bold fonts are generally used for emphasis. Italics should be used for titles of longer works, such as novels, movies, books, magazines, and plays. They are also used to denote a foreign word or phrase. Note that italicized fonts and underlined fonts serve similar purposes and are often used interchangeably. Underlining is more commonly used in handwritten documents.

Example

13. Which of the following sentences properly uses italics?

A) We enjoyed our vacation in *Sacramento, California*.

B) Adam ate two plates of *pasta with meatballs*.

C) Angela's favorite book is *The Art of War*.

D) The traffic on *Main Street* is terrible during rush hour.

ANSWER KEY

1. **B) Correct.** Computers account for 62 percent of sales. Mobile phones (choice A) are 21 percent, software and tablets (choice C) equal 17 percent, and software and mobile phones (choice D) equal 28 percent.

2. **C) Correct.** Mobile phones (21 percent) and tablets (10 percent) together account for 31 percent of Wholesale Electronics' total sales.

3. **D) Correct.** Ruby Stone Lake is north of Park Headquarters.

4. **C) Correct.** Using the distance scale, it is possible to estimate that the center of Tananite Forest is approximately 4 miles from the state monument.

5. **C) Correct.** The notation %SpO$_2$ stands for oxygen saturation, which reads 100 percent.

6. **A) Correct.** The EKG monitor shows a systolic reading of 100, which places the patient in the Normal category.

7. **A) Correct.** When you add the base price, shipping and handling fees, and taxes, shoes from Famous Shoes cost $84.88, so Rachel can only shop at Wholesale Footwear ($78.62) and Bargain Sales ($77.32).

8. **A) Correct.** Bargain Sales and Famous Shoes are both under Allen's budget for taxes and shipping and handling.

9. **B) Correct.** Starting with 3 red apples and 1 green apple, and following the directions, you have:
   1. 2 red apples and 1 green apple
   2. 2 red apples and 2 green apples
   3. 3 red apples and 2 green apples
   4. 3 red apples and 3 green apples
   5. 1 red apple and 3 green apples
   6. 1 red apple and 2 green apples
   7. 4 red apples and 2 green apples
   8. 4 red apples and 4 green apples

10. **C) Correct.** Starting with 12 gallons, and following the directions, you have:
   1. 11 gallons
   2. 10 gallons
   3. 9.5 gallons
   4. 9 gallons
   5. 7 gallons

11. **A) Correct.** According to the index, this information can be found between pages 237 and 291.

12. C) Correct. According to the table of contents, page 125 is in Chapter 3: Geometry.

13. C) Correct. The sentence in choice C italicizes the title of a longer work and is therefore correct. Italics are not used for names of cities (choice A), foods (choice B), or streets (choice D).

3

WORKPLACE DOCUMENTS: READING

The Workplace Documents Assessment on the ACT WorkKeys® will require you to read nonfiction passages related to workplace issues and then answer questions about them. These questions will fall into three categories:

KEY IDEAS AND DETAILS questions ask about the main idea of the passage and the details that support that main idea.

CRAFT AND STRUCTURE questions ask about the craft of writing, including organization of the text, word choice, and the author's purpose.

INTEGRATION OF KNOWLEDGE AND IDEAS questions require drawing conclusions from passages and integrating information from multiple sources.

THE MAIN IDEA

The **MAIN IDEA** of a text is the argument that the author is trying to make about a particular **TOPIC**. Every sentence in a passage should support or address the main idea in some way.

Identifying the Main Idea

Consider a political election. A candidate is running for office and plans to deliver a speech asserting her position on tax reform, which is that taxes should be lowered. The topic of the speech is tax reform, and the main idea is that taxes should be lowered. The candidate is going to assert this in her speech, and support it with examples proving why lowering taxes would benefit the public and how it could be accomplished.

> ⚠️
> **Topic:** The subject of the passage. **Main idea:** The argument the writer is making about the topic.

Other candidates may have different perspectives on the same topic; they may believe that higher taxes are necessary, or that current taxes are adequate. It is likely that their speeches, while on the same topic of tax reform, would have different main ideas supported by different examples and evidence.

Let's look at an example passage to see how to identify the topic and main idea.

Babe Didrikson Zaharias, one of the most decorated female athletes of the twentieth century, is an inspiration for everyone. Born in 1911 in Beaumont, Texas, Zaharias lived in a time when women were considered second class to men, but she never let that stop her from becoming a champion. Zaharias was one of seven children in a poor immigrant family and was competitive from an early age. As a child she excelled at most things she tried, especially sports, which continued into high school and beyond. After high school, Zaharias played amateur basketball for two years, and soon after began training in track and field. Despite the fact that women were only allowed to enter in three events, Zaharias represented the United States in the 1932 Los Angeles Olympics, and won two gold medals and one silver in track and field events.

The topic of this paragraph is obviously Babe Zaharias—the whole passage describes events from her life. Determining the main idea, however, requires a little more analysis. To figure out the main idea, consider what the writer is saying about Zaharias. The passage describes her life, but the main idea of the paragraph is what it says about her accomplishments. The writer is saying that she is someone to admire. That is the main idea and what unites all the information in the paragraph.

Example

From so far away it's easy to imagine the surface of our solar system's planets as enigmas—how could we ever know what those far-flung planets really look like? It turns out, however, that scientists have a number of tools at their disposal that allow them to paint detailed pictures of many planets' surfaces. The topography of Venus, for example, has been explored by several space probes, including the Russian Venera landers and NASA's *Magellan* orbiter. In addition to these long-range probes, NASA has also used its series of "Great Observatories" to study distant planets. These four massively powerful orbiting telescopes are the famous Hubble Space Telescope, the Compton Gamma Ray Observatory, the Chandra X-Ray Observatory, and the Spitzer Space Telescope. Such powerful telescopes aren't just found in space: NASA makes use of Earth-based telescopes as well. Scientists at the National Radio Astronomy Observatory in Charlottesville, Virginia, have spent decades using radio imaging to build an incredibly detailed portrait of Venus's surface.

1.   Which of the following sentences best describes the main idea of the passage?

     A) It's impossible to know what the surfaces of other planets are really like.

     B) Telescopes are an important tool for scientists studying planets in our solar system.

     C) Venus's surface has many of the same features as Earth's, including volcanoes, craters, and channels.

     D) Scientists use a variety of advanced technologies to study the surfaces of the planets in our solar system.

Topic and Summary Sentences

The topic, and sometimes the main idea of a paragraph, is introduced in the TOPIC SENTENCE. The topic sentence usually appears early in a passage. The first sentence in the example paragraph about Babe Zaharias states the topic and main idea: *Babe Didrikson Zaharias, one of the most decorated female athletes of the twentieth century, is an inspiration for everyone.*

Even though paragraphs generally begin with topic sentences, on occasion writers build up to the topic sentence by using supporting details in order to generate interest or construct an argument. Be alert for paragraphs in which writers do not include a clear topic sentence.

There may also be a SUMMARY SENTENCE at the end of a passage. As its name suggests, this sentence sums up the passage, often by restating the main idea and the author's key evidence supporting it.

Example

The Constitution of the United States establishes a series of limits to rein in centralized power. "Separation of powers" distributes federal authority among three branches: the executive, the legislative, and the judicial. "Checks and balances" allow the branches to prevent any one branch from usurping power. "States' rights" are protected under the Constitution from too much encroachment by the federal government. "Enumeration of powers" names the specific and few powers the federal government has. These four restrictions have helped sustain the American republic for over two centuries.

2. Which of the following is the passage's topic sentence?

   A) These four restrictions have helped sustain the American republic for over two centuries.

   B) The Constitution of the United States establishes a series of limits to rein in centralized power.

   C) "Enumeration of powers" names the specific and few powers the federal government has.

   D) "Checks and balances" allow the branches to prevent any one branch from usurping power.

SUPPORTING DETAILS

SUPPORTING DETAILS reinforce the author's main idea. Let's look again at the passage about athlete Babe Zaharias.

Babe Didrikson Zaharias, one of the most decorated female athletes of the twentieth century, is an inspiration for everyone. Born in 1911 in Beaumont, Texas, Zaharias lived in a time when women were considered second class to men, but she never let that stop her from becoming a champion. Babe was one of seven children in a poor immigrant family and was competitive from an early age. As a child she excelled at most things she tried, especially sports, which continued into high school and beyond. After high school, Babe played amateur basketball for two years, and soon after began training in track and field. Despite the fact that women were only allowed to enter in three events, Zaharias represented the United States in the 1932 Los Angeles Olympics, and won two gold medals and one silver for track and field events.

Remember that the main idea of the passage is that Zaharias is someone to admire—an idea introduced in the opening sentence. The remainder of the paragraph provides details that support this assertion. These details include the circumstances of her childhood, her childhood success at sports, and the medals she won at the Olympics.

When looking for supporting details, be alert for SIGNAL WORDS. These signal words tell you that a supporting fact or idea will follow, and so can be helpful in identifying supporting details. Signal words can also help you rule out certain sentences as the main idea or topic sentence. If a sentence begins with one of these phrases, it will likely be too specific to be a main idea.

Examples

From so far away it's easy to imagine the surface of our solar system's planets as enigmas—how could we ever know what those far-flung planets really look like? It turns out, however, that scientists have a number of tools at their disposal that allow them to paint detailed pictures of many planets' surfaces. The topography of Venus, for example, has been explored by several space probes, including the Russian Venera landers and NASA's *Magellan* orbiter. In addition to these long-range probes, NASA has also used its series of orbiting telescopes to study distant planets. These four massively powerful telescopes include the famous Hubble Space Telescope as well as the Compton Gamma Ray Observatory, the Chandra X-Ray Observatory, and the Spitzer Space Telescope. Such powerful telescopes aren't just found in space: NASA makes use of Earth-based telescopes as well. Scientists at the National Radio Astronomy Observatory in Charlottesville, Virginia, have spent decades using radio imaging to build an incredibly detailed portrait of Venus's surface.

3. According to the passage, which of the following is a space probe used to explore the surface of Venus?

   A) *Magellan* orbiter

   B) Hubble Space Telescope

   C) Spitzer Space Telescope

   D) National Radio Astronomy Observatory

4. If true, which detail could be added to the passage above to support the author's argument that scientists use many different technologies to study the surface of planets?

   A) Because Earth's atmosphere blocks X-rays, gamma rays, and infrared radiation, NASA needed to put telescopes in orbit above the atmosphere.

   B) In 2015, NASA released a map of Venus that was created by compiling images from orbiting telescopes and long-range space probes.

   C) NASA is currently using the *Curiosity* and *Opportunity* rovers to look for signs of ancient life on Mars.

   D) NASA has spent over $2.5 billion to build, launch, and repair the Hubble Space Telescope.

FACTS VERSUS OPINIONS

On the ACT WorkKeys® Workplace Documents Assessment, you might be asked to identify a statement as either a fact or an opinion. A FACT is a statement or thought that can be proven to be true. The statement *Wednesday comes after Tuesday* is a fact—you can point to a calendar to prove it. In contrast, an OPINION is an assumption, not based in fact, that cannot be proven to be true. The assertion that *television is more entertaining than feature films* is an opinion—people will disagree on this, and there is no reference you can use to prove or disprove it.

Example

Exercise is critical for healthy development in children. Today in the United States, there is an epidemic of poor childhood health; many of these children will face further illnesses in adulthood that are due to poor diet and lack of exercise now. This is a problem for all Americans, especially with the rising cost of health care.

It is vital that school systems and parents encourage children to engage in a minimum of thirty minutes of cardiovascular exercise each day, mildly increasing their heart rate for a sustained period. This is proven to decrease the likelihood of developmental diabetes, obesity, and a multitude of other health problems. Also, children need a proper diet, rich in fruits and vegetables, so they can develop physically and learn healthy eating habits early on.

5. Which of the following in the passage is a fact, not an opinion?
   A) Fruits and vegetables are the best way to help children be healthy.
   B) Children today are lazier than they were in previous generations.
   C) The risk of diabetes in children is reduced by physical activity.
   D) Children should engage in thirty minutes of exercise a day.

MAKING INFERENCES

In addition to understanding the main idea and factual content of a passage, you will also be asked to take your analysis one step further and anticipate what other information could logically be added to the passage. In a nonfiction passage, for example, you might be asked which statement the author of the passage would agree with. In an excerpt from a fictional work, you might be asked to anticipate what the character would do next.

To answer such questions, you need to have a solid understanding of the topic and main idea of the passage. Armed with this information, you can figure out which of the answer choices best fits the criteria (or, alternatively, which do not). For example, if the author of the passage is advocating for safer working conditions in factories, any details that could be added to the passage should support that idea. You might add sentences that contain information about the number of accidents that occur in factories or that outline a new plan for fire safety.

Example

Exercise is critical for healthy development in children. Today in the United States, there is an epidemic of poor childhood health; many of these children will face further illnesses in adulthood that are due to poor diet and lack of exercise now. This is a problem for all Americans, especially with the rising cost of health care.

It is vital that school systems and parents encourage children to engage in a minimum of thirty minutes of cardiovascular exercise each day, mildly increasing their heart rate for a sustained period. This is proven to decrease the likelihood of developmental diabetes, obesity, and a multitude of other health problems. Also, children need a proper diet, rich in fruits and vegetables, so they can develop physically and learn healthy eating habits early on.

6. Which of the following statements might the author of this passage agree with?

  A) Adults who do not have healthy eating habits should be forced to pay more for health care.

  B) Schools should be required by federal law to provide vegetables with every meal.

  C) Healthy eating habits can only be learned at home.

  D) Schools should encourage students to bring lunches from home.

TYPES OF PASSAGES

Authors typically write with a purpose. Sometimes referred to as "authorial intention," an author's purpose lets us know why the author is writing and what he or she would like to accomplish. There are many reasons an author might write, but most write for one of four reasons:

- to ENTERTAIN the reader or tell a story
- to PERSUADE the reader of his or her opinion
- to DESCRIBE something, such as a person, place, thing, or event
- to EXPLAIN a process or procedure

Identifying an author's purpose can be tricky, but the writing itself often gives clues. For example, if an author's purpose is to entertain, the writing may include vivid characters, exciting plot twists, or beautiful, figurative language. On the other hand, if an author wishes to persuade the reader, the passage may present an argument or contain convincing examples that support the author's point of view. An author who wishes to describe a person, place, or event may include lots of details as well as plenty of adjectives and adverbs. Finally, the author whose purpose is to explain a process or procedure may include step-by-step instructions or might present information in a sequence.

Related to authorial intention, described above, are the different MODES of written materials. A short story, for example, is meant to entertain, while an online news article is designed to inform the public about a current event.

Each of these different types of writing has a specific name. On the ACT WorkKeys® Workplace Documents Assessment, most documents fall into one of these three categories:

- INFORMATIONAL (or EXPOSITORY) WRITING informs people (newspaper and magazine articles).
- TECHNICAL WRITING explains something (product manual, instructions).
- PERSUASIVE WRITING tries to convince the reader of something (opinion column or a blog).

Examples

One of my summer reading books was *Mockingjay*. I was captivated by the adventures of the main character and the complicated plot of the book. However, I would argue that the ending didn't reflect the excitement of the story. Given what a powerful personality the main character has, I felt like the ending didn't do her justice.

7. Which of the following best captures the author's purpose?

    A) explain the plot of the novel *Mockingjay*

    B) persuade the reader that the ending of *Mockingjay* is inferior

    C) list the novels she read during the summer

    D) explain why the ending of a novel is important

Elizabeth closed her eyes and braced herself on the armrests that divided her from her fellow passengers. Takeoff was always the worst part for her. The revving of the engines, the way her stomach dropped as the plane lurched upward: It made her feel sick. Then, she had to watch the world fade away beneath her, getting smaller and smaller until it was just her and the clouds hurtling through the sky. Sometimes (but only sometimes) it just had to be endured. She focused on the thought of her sister's smiling face and her new baby nephew as the plane slowly pulled onto the runway.

8. Which of the following best describes the mode of the passage?

    A) narrative

    B) expository

    C) technical

    D) persuasive

TEXT STRUCTURE

Authors can structure passages in a number of different ways. These distinct organizational patterns, referred to as **TEXT STRUCTURE**, use the logical relationships between ideas to improve the readability and coherence of a text. The most common ways passages are organized include:

- **PROBLEM-SOLUTION:** The author outlines a problem and then discusses a solution.

- **COMPARISON-CONTRAST:** The author presents two situations and then discusses the similarities and differences.

- **CAUSE-EFFECT:** The author recounts an action and then discusses the resulting effects.

- **DESCRIPTIVE:** The author describes an idea, object, person, or other item in detail.

Example

The issue of public transportation has begun to haunt the fast-growing cities of the southern United States. Unlike their northern counterparts, cities like Atlanta, Dallas, and Houston have long promoted growth out and not up—these are cities full of sprawling suburbs and single-family homes, not densely concentrated skyscrapers and apartment buildings. What to do then, when all those suburbanites need to get into the central business districts for work? For a long time it seemed highways were the answer: twenty-lane–wide expanses of concrete that would allow commuters to move from home to work and back again. But these modern miracles have become time-sucking, pollution-spewing nightmares. The residents of these cities may not like it, but it's time for them to turn toward public transport like trains and buses if they want their cities to remain livable.

9. The organization of this passage can best be described as:
   A) a comparison of two similar ideas.
   B) a description of a place.
   C) a discussion of several effects all related to the same cause.
   D) a discussion of a problem followed by a suggested solution.

VOCABULARY

On the Workplace Documents Assessment, you may also be asked to provide definitions or intended meanings of words within passages. You may have never encountered some of these words before the test, but there are tricks you can use to figure out what they mean.

Context Clues

One of the most fundamental vocabulary skills is using the context in which a word is found to determine its meaning. Your ability to read sentences carefully is extremely helpful when it comes to understanding new vocabulary words.

Vocabulary questions on the Workplace Documents Assessment will usually include SENTENCE CONTEXT CLUES within the sentence that contains the word. There are several clues that can help you understand the context, and therefore the meaning of a word:

RESTATEMENT CLUES state the definition of the word in the sentence. The definition is often set apart from the rest of the sentence by a comma, parentheses, or a colon.

> Teachers often prefer teaching students with intrinsic motivation: these students have an internal desire to learn.
>
> The meaning of *intrinsic* is restated as *internal*.

CONTRAST CLUES include the opposite meaning of a word. Words like *but*, *on the other hand*, and *however* are tip-offs that a sentence contains a contrast clue.

> Janet was destitute after she lost her job, but her wealthy sister helped her get back on her feet.
>
> *Destitute* is contrasted with *wealthy*, so the definition of destitute is *poor*.

POSITIVE/NEGATIVE CLUES tell you whether a word has a positive or negative meaning.

> The film was lauded by critics as stunning, and was nominated for several awards.
>
> The positive descriptions *stunning* and *nominated for several awards* suggest that *lauded* has a positive meaning.

Examples

Select the answer that most closely matches the definition of the underlined word or phrase as it is used in the sentence.

10. The dog was dauntless in the face of danger, braving the fire to save the girl trapped inside the building.

A) difficult

B) fearless

C) imaginative

D) startled

11. Beth did not spend any time preparing for the test, but Tyrone kept a <u>rigorous</u> study schedule.

A) strict

B) loose

C) boring

D) strange

Analyzing Words

As you know, determining the meaning of a word can be more complicated than just looking in a dictionary. A word might have more than one DENOTATION, or definition, and which one the author intends can only be judged by looking at the surrounding text. For example, the word *quack* can refer to the sound a duck makes or to a person who publicly pretends to have a qualification which they do not actually possess.

A word may also have different CONNOTATIONS, which are the implied meanings and emotions a word evokes in the reader. For example, a cubicle is simply a walled desk in an office, but for many the word implies a constrictive, uninspiring workplace. Connotations can vary greatly between cultures and even between individuals.

Finally, authors might make use of FIGURATIVE LANGUAGE, which is the use of a word to imply something other than the word's literal definition. This is often done by comparing two things. If you say *I felt like a butterfly when I got a new haircut*, the listener knows you do not resemble an insect but instead felt beautiful and transformed.

Examples

Select the answer that most closely matches the definition of the underlined word or phrase as it is used in the sentence.

12. The patient's uneven <u>pupils</u> suggested that brain damage was possible.

A) part of the eye

B) student in a classroom

C) walking pace

D) breathing sounds

13. Aiden examined the antique lamp and worried that he had been <u>taken for a ride</u>. He had paid a lot for the vintage lamp, but it looked like it was worthless.

A) transported

B) forgotten

C) deceived

D) hindered

Word Structure

You are not expected to know every word in the English language for your test; rather, you will need to use deductive reasoning to find the best definition of the word in question. Many words can be broken down into three main parts to help determine their meaning:

PREFIX — ROOT — SUFFIX

ROOTS are the building blocks of all words. Every word is either a root itself or has a root. The root is what is left when you strip away the prefixes and suffixes from a word. For example, in the word *unclear*, if you take away the prefix *un–*, you have the root *clear*.

Roots are not always recognizable words, because they often come from Latin or Greek words, such as *nat*, a Latin root meaning born. The word *native*, which means a person born in a referenced place, comes from this root; so does the word *prenatal*, meaning *before birth*. It is important to keep in mind, however, that roots do not always match the original definitions of words, and they can have several different spellings.

PREFIXES are elements added to the beginning of a word, and **SUFFIXES** are elements added to the end of the word; together they are known as affixes. They carry assigned meanings and can be attached to a word to completely change the word's meaning or to enhance the word's original meaning.

> ✔
> Can you figure out the definitions of the following words using their parts? *ambidextrous, anthropology, diagram, egocentric, hemisphere, homicide, metamorphosis, nonsense, portable, rewind, submarine, triangle, unicycle*

Let's use the word *prefix* itself as an example: *fix* means to place something securely and *pre–* means before. Therefore, *prefix* means to place something before or in front of. Now let's look at a suffix: in the word *feminism*, *femin* is a root which means female. The suffix *–ism* means act, practice, or process. Thus, *feminism* is the process of establishing equal rights for women.

Although you cannot determine the meaning of a word from a prefix or suffix alone, you can use this knowledge to eliminate answer choices. Understanding whether the word is positive or negative can give you the partial meaning of the word.

Table 3.1. Common Roots

ROOT	DEFINITION	EXAMPLE
ast(er)	star	asteroid, astronomy
audi	hear	audience, audible
auto	self	automatic, autograph
bene	good	beneficent, benign
bio	life	biology, biorhythm
cap	take	capture
ced	yield	secede
chrono	time	chronometer, chronic
corp	body	corporeal
crac or crat	rule	autocrat
demo	people	democracy
dict	say	dictionary, dictation

ROOT	DEFINITION	EXAMPLE
duc	lead or make	ductile, produce
gen	give birth	generation, genetics
geo	earth	geography, geometry
grad	step	graduate
graph	write	graphical, autograph
ject	throw	eject
jur or jus	law	justice, jurisdiction
juven	young	juvenile
log or logue	thought	logic, logarithm
luc	light	lucidity
man	hand	manual
mand	order	remand
mis	send	transmission
mono	one	monotone
omni	all	omnivore
path	feel	sympathy
phil	love	philanthropy
phon	sound	phonograph
port	carry	export
qui	rest	quiet
scrib or script	write	scribe, transcript
sense or sent	feel	sentiment
tele	far away	telephone
terr	earth	terrace
uni	single	unicode
vac	empty	vacant
vid or vis	see	video, vision

Table 3.2. Common Prefixes

PREFIX	DEFINITION	EXAMPLE
a– (also an–)	not, without; to, toward; of, completely	atheist, anemic, aside, aback, anew, abashed
ante–	before, preceding	antecedent, anteroom
anti–	opposing, against	antibiotic, anticlimax
belli–	warlike, combative	belligerent, bellicose
com– (also co–, col–, con–, cor–)	with, jointly, completely	combat, cooperate, collide, confide, correspond
dis– (also di–)	negation, removal	disadvantage, disbar

Table 3.2. Common Prefixes (continued)

PREFIX	DEFINITION	EXAMPLE
en– (also em–)	put into or on; bring into the condition of; intensify	engulf, embrace
hypo–	under	hypoglycemic, hypodermic
in– (also il–, im–, ir–)	not, without; in, into, toward, inside	infertile, impossible, illegal, irregular, influence, include
intra–	inside, within	intravenous, intrapersonal
out–	surpassing, exceeding; external, away from	outperform, outdoor
over–	excessively, completely; upper, outer, over, above	overconfident, overcast
pre–	before	precondition, preadolescent, prelude
re–	again	reapply, remake
semi–	half, partly	semicircle, semiconscious
syn– (also sym–)	in union, acting together	synthesis, symbiotic
trans–	across, beyond	transdermal
trans–	into a different state	translate
under–	beneath, below; not enough	underarm, undersecretary, underdeveloped

Examples

Select the answer that most closely matches the definition of the underlined word or phrase as it is used in the sentence.

14. The <u>bellicose</u> dog will be sent to training school next week.
    A) misbehaved
    B) friendly
    C) scared
    D) aggressive

15. The new menu <u>rejuvenated</u> the restaurant and made it one of the most popular spots in town.
    A) established
    B) invigorated
    C) improved
    D) motivated

1. **D) Correct.** Choice A can be eliminated because it directly contradicts the rest of the passage. Choices B and C can also be eliminated because they offer only specific details from the passage. While both choices contain details from the passage, neither is general enough to encompass the passage as a whole. Only choice D provides an assertion that is both backed up by the passage's content and general enough to cover the entire passage.

2. **B) Correct.** Choice B is the first sentence of the passage and introduces the topic. Choice A is the final sentence of the passage and summarizes the passage's content. Choices C and D are supporting sentences found within the body of the passage. They include important details that support the main idea of the passage.

3. **A) Correct.** The passage states, "The topography of Venus, for example, has been explored by several space probes, including the Russian Venera landers and NASA's *Magellan* orbiter." The other choices are mentioned in the passage, but are not space probes.

4. **B) Correct.** Choice B is the best option because it addresses the use of multiple technologies to study the surface of planets. Choices C and D can be eliminated because they do not address the topic of studying the surface of planets. Choice A can also be eliminated because it only addresses a single technology.

5. **C) Correct.** Choice C is a simple fact stated by the author. It is introduced by the word *proven* to indicate that it is supported by evidence. Choice B can be discarded immediately because it is not discussed anywhere in the passage, and also because it is negative, usually a hint in multiple-choice questions that an answer choice is wrong. Choices A and D are both opinions—the author is promoting exercise, fruits, and vegetables as a way to make children healthy. (Notice that these incorrect answers contain words that hint at being an opinion such as *best* or *should*.)

6. **B) Correct.** Since the author argues that children need a proper diet rich in fruits and vegetables, we can infer that the author would agree with choice B. The author describes the cost of health care as a problem for all Americans, implying that he would not want to punish adults who never learned healthy eating habits (choice A). Choices C and D are contradicted by the author's focus on creating healthy habits in schools.

7. **B) Correct.** The purpose of the above passage is to persuade the reader of the author's opinion of the novel *Mockingjay*, specifically that the ending did not do the main character justice. The passage's use of the verb "argue" tells us that the passage is presenting a case to the reader. The passage follows this statement with evidence—that the main character had a powerful personality.

8. **A) Correct.** The passage is telling a story—we meet Elizabeth and learn about her fear of flying—so it is a narrative text. There is no factual information presented or explained, nor is the author trying to persuade the reader.

9. **D) Correct.** Choice C is wrong because the author provides no root cause or a list of effects. Choices A and B are tricky, because the passage contains structures similar to those described above. For example, it compares two things (cities in the North and

South) and describes a place (a sprawling city). However, if you look at the overall organization of the passage, you can see that it starts by presenting a problem (transportation) and then suggests a solution (trains and buses), making answer D the only choice that encompasses the entire passage.

10. **B) Correct.** Demonstrating bravery in the face of danger would be fearless. The restatement clue (*braving*) tells you exactly what the word means.

11. **A) Correct.** The word *but* tells us that Tyrone studied in a different way from Beth, which means it is a contrast clue. If Beth did not study hard, then Tyrone did. The best answer, therefore, is choice A.

12. **A) Correct.** Only choice A matches both the definition of the word and context of the sentence. Choice B is an alternative definition for pupil, but does not make sense in the sentence. Both C and D could be correct in the context of the sentence, but neither is a definition of pupil.

13. **C) Correct.** It is clear from the context of the sentence that Aiden was not literally taken for a ride. Instead, this phrase is an example of figurative language. From context clues you can figure out that Aiden paid too much for the lamp, so he was deceived.

14. **D) Correct.** Both *misbehaved* and *aggressive* look like possible answers given the context of the sentence. However, the prefix *belli–*, which means warlike, can be used to confirm that *aggressive* is the right answer.

15. **B) Correct.** All the answer choices could make sense in the context of the sentence, so it is necessary to use word structure to find the definition. The root *juven* means young and the prefix *re–* means again, so *rejuvenate* means to be made young again. The answer choice with the most similar meaning is *invigorated*, which means to give something energy.

4

PRACTICE TEST

APPLIED MATHEMATICS

Work the problem, and then choose the most correct answer.

1. If a person reads 40 pages in 45 minutes, approximately how many minutes will it take her to read 265 pages?

    A) 202
    B) 236
    C) 265
    D) 298
    E) 300

2. The population of a town was 7,250 in 2014 and 7,375 in 2015. What was the percent increase from 2014 to 2015 to the nearest tenth of a percent?

    A) 1.5%
    B) 1.6%
    C) 1.7%
    D) 1.8%
    E) 2.0%

3. Which of the following has the greatest value?

    A) $20 - (-20)$
    B) $-16 - 17 + 31$
    C) $18 - 15 + 27$
    D) $-20 + 10 + 10$
    E) $-4(3)(-2)$

4. Simplify: $(4.71 \times 10^3) - (2.98 \times 10^2)$

    A) 1.73×10
    B) 4.412×10^2
    C) 1.73×10^3
    D) -14.038×10^5
    E) 4.412×10^3

5. Simplify: $(1.2 \times 10^{-3})(1.13 \times 10^{-4})$

    A) 1.356×10^{-12}
    B) 1.356×10^{-7}
    C) 1.356×10^{-1}
    D) 1.356×10
    E) 1.356×10^{12}

6. Simplify: $-(3^2) + (5 - 7)^2 - 3(4 - 8)$

    A) -25
    B) -17
    C) -1
    D) 7
    E) 25

7. Simplify: $(3^2 \div 1^3) - (4 - 8^2) + 2^4$

    A) -35
    B) -4
    C) 9
    D) 28
    E) 85

8. Simplify: $17.38 - 19.26 + 14.2$

A) 12.08

B) 12.32

C) 16.08

D) 16.22

E) 50.84

9. Simplify: $\frac{7}{8} - \frac{1}{10} - \frac{2}{3}$

A) $\frac{1}{30}$

B) $\frac{4}{120}$

C) $\frac{13}{120}$

D) $\frac{4}{21}$

E) $\frac{4}{105}$

10. Simplify: $\left(1\frac{1}{2}\right)\left(2\frac{2}{3}\right) \div \left(1\frac{1}{4}\right)$

A) $3\frac{1}{12}$

B) $3\frac{1}{5}$

C) 4

D) 5

E) $5\frac{3}{12}$

11. Convert 3.28 to a fraction.

A) $3\frac{1}{50}$

B) $3\frac{1}{25}$

C) $3\frac{7}{50}$

D) $3\frac{4}{25}$

E. $3\frac{7}{25}$

12. Which of the following is listed in order from least to greatest?

A) $-0.95, 0, \frac{2}{5}, 0.35, \frac{3}{4}$

B) $-1, -\frac{1}{10}, -0.11, \frac{5}{6}, 0.75$

C) $-\frac{3}{4}, -0.2, 0, \frac{2}{3}, 0.55$

D) $-1.1, -\frac{4}{5}, -0.13, 0.7, \frac{9}{11}$

E) $-0.0001, -\frac{1}{12}, 0, \frac{2}{3}, \frac{4}{5}$

13. Convert 8 pounds, 8 ounces to kilograms to the nearest tenth of a kilogram.

A) 3.9 kilograms

B) 4.1 kilograms

C) 17.6 kilograms

D) 18.7 kilograms

E) 19.36 kilograms

14. What is the remainder when 397 is divided by 4?

A) 0

B) 1

C) 2

D) 3

E) 4

15. What is 498,235 rounded to the nearest thousands?

A) 498,000

B) 498,200

C) 499,000

D) 499,200

E) 500,000

16. Allison used $2\frac{1}{2}$ cups of flour to make a cake, and $\frac{3}{4}$ of a cup of flour to make a pie. If she started with 4 cups of flour, how many cups of flour does she have left?

A) $\frac{3}{4}$

B) 1

C) $\frac{5}{4}$

D) $\frac{5}{2}$

E) $\frac{13}{4}$

17. Michael is making cupcakes. He plans to give $\frac{1}{2}$ of the cupcakes to a friend and $\frac{1}{3}$ of the cupcakes to his coworkers. If he makes 48 cupcakes, how many will he have left over?

A) 8

B) 10

C) 12

D) 16

E) 24

18. Aprille has $50 to buy the items on her shopping list. Assuming there is no sales tax, about how much change will Aprille receive after buying all the items on her list?

Aprille's List

ITEM	PRICE
Hammer	$13.24
Screwdriver	$11.99
Nails	$4.27
Wrench	$5.60

A) $12
B) $13
C) $14
D) $15
E) $16

19. Students board a bus at 7:45 a.m. and arrive at school at 8:20 a.m. How long are the students on the bus?

A) 30 minutes
B) 35 minutes
C) 45 minutes
D) 50 minutes
E) 65 minutes

20. Out of 1560 students at Ward Middle School, 15% want to take French. Which expression represents how many students want to take French?

A) $1560 \div 15$
B) 1560×15
C) 1560×0.15
D) $1560 \div 0.15$
E) 1560×1.5

21. What is the percent increase in an employee's salary if it is raised from $57,000 to $60,000?

A) 0.3%
B) 0.4%
C) 3%
D) 4%
E) 5%

22. If a car uses 8 gallons of gas to travel 650 miles, how many miles can it travel using 12 gallons of gas?

A) 870 miles
B) 895 miles
C) 915 miles
D) 975 miles
E) 1,025 miles

23. At the grocery store, apples cost $1.89 per pound and oranges cost $2.19 per pound. How much would it cost to purchase 2 pounds of apples and 1.5 pounds of oranges?

A) $6.62
B) $7.07
C) $7.14
D) $7.22
E) $7.67

24. A bike store is having a 30%-off sale, and one of the bikes is on sale for $385. What was the original price of this bike?

A) $253.00
B) $450.00
C) $500.50
D) $550.00
E) $600.00

25. Which statement about the following set is true?
{60, 5, 18, 20, 37, 37, 11, 90, 72}

A) The median and the mean are equal.
B) The mean is less than the mode.
C) The mode is greater than the median.
D) The median is less than the mean.
E) The mode and the mean are equal.

26. Some of a hotel's 400 rooms have an ocean view and the rest of the rooms do not. If the probability of getting a room with an ocean view is 35%, how many rooms do NOT have an ocean view?

A) 65
B) 140
C) 200
D) 260
E) 300

Use the following graph for questions 27 and 28.

Number of Months with 3 or Fewer Than 3 Inches of Rain

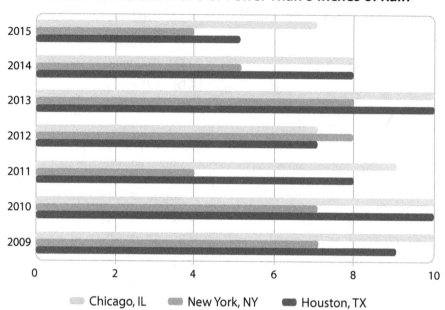

Chicago, IL   New York, NY   Houston, TX

27. New York had the fewest months with less than 3 inches of rain in every year except:

A) 2011

B) 2012

C) 2013

D) 2014

E) 2015

28. From 2009 to 2015, what is the average number of months that Chicago had 3 or less inches of rain?

A) 5

B) 6

C) 7

D) 8

E) 9

29. In the fall, 425 students pass the math benchmark. In the spring, 680 students pass the same benchmark. What is the percentage increase in passing scores from fall to spring?

A) 37.5%

B) 55%

C) 60%

D) 62.5%

E) 80%

30. The pie graph below shows how a state's government plans to spend its annual budget of $3 billion. How much more money does the state plan to spend on infrastructure than education?

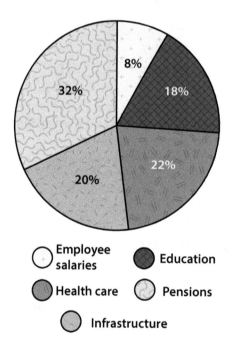

Employee salaries   Education

Health care   Pensions

Infrastructure

A) $60,000,000

B) $120,000,000

C) $300,000,000

D) $540,000,000

E) $600,000,000

31. Which conclusion can be drawn from the graph?

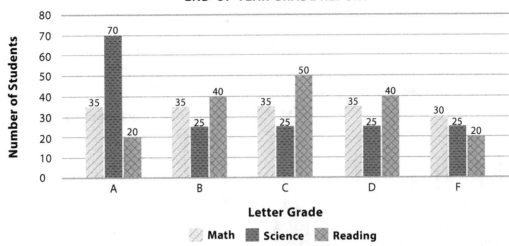

END-OF-YEAR GRADE REPORT

A) More than twice as many students earned an A in science than earned an F in science.

B) The majority of the students earned a C in math.

C) The number of students who earned a B in reading is equal to the number of students who earned a B in math.

D) Next year's students will not need intensive science instruction.

E) More students earned a C in science than earned a D in science.

32. What is the area of the shape?

A) 6 mm²

B) 16 mm²

C) 64 mm²

D) 128 mm²

E) 144 mm²

33. An ice chest contains 24 sodas, some regular and some diet. The ratio of diet soda to regular soda is 1:3. How many regular sodas are there in the ice chest?

A) 1

B) 4

C) 6

D) 18

E) 24

34. A person earning a salary between $75,000 and $100,000 per year will pay $10,620 in taxes plus 20% of any amount over $75,000. What would a person earning $80,000 per year pay in taxes?

A) $10,620

B) $11,620

C) $12,120

D) $12,744

E) $15,620

GRAPHIC LITERACY

Study the image or passage closely, and then answer the following questions.

Questions 1 – 3 refer to the figure below, a blood pressure monitor.

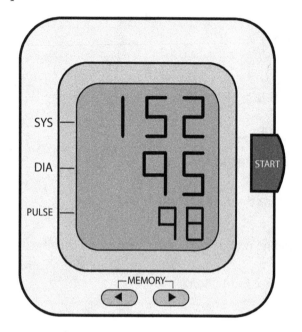

The next questions refer to the graph below depicting Alex's income from her business, Alex's Babysitting Service.

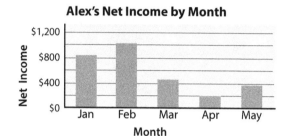

1. The figure above represents a blood pressure monitor. Which of the following represents the systolic blood pressure reading?

   A) 152

   B) 95

   C) 98

   D) 152/95

2. On the blood pressure monitor above, which of the following represents the diastolic blood pressure reading?

   A) 152

   B) 95

   C) 98

   D) 152/95

3. On the blood pressure monitor, which of the following represents the pulse reading?

   A) 152

   B) 95

   C) 98

   D) 152/95

4. Based on the information in the graph, about how much more money did Alex bring in during February than during April?

   A) $200

   B) $800

   C) $1,100

   D) $1,300

5. Based on the information in the graph, did Alex's Babysitting Service bring in more money in February and March combined or in January, April, and May combined? About how much difference was there?

   A) about $100 more in February and March than in January, April, and May

   B) about $200 more in February and March than in January, April, and May

   C) about $100 more in January, April, and May than in February and March

   D) about $200 more in January, April, and May than in February and March

The consumer price index (CPI) measures prices of goods and services as they change over time. Economists select a "base year" and compile a market "basket" of 400 consumer goods and services (like gas, appliances, and groceries) from that year. They create the price index by measuring the change in prices.

The graph below shows a sample of the CPI in the United States between 1913 and 2010. The dark line shows the average CPI for each year, with 1982 – 1984 as the "base year" (when CPI = 100).

The numbers on the left represent the CPI, ranging from 0 to 250. The percentages on the right represent levels of increase or decrease beyond the CPI of the base year.

The light line ("Change in Average Consumer Price Index") represents the percent change in average CPI from year to year.

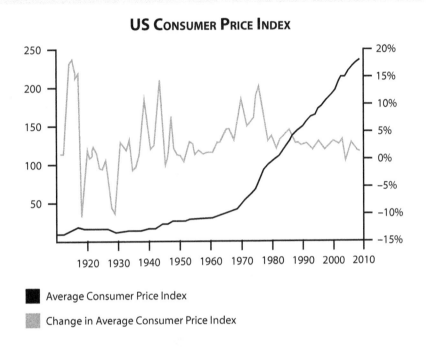

US CONSUMER PRICE INDEX

■ Average Consumer Price Index

▓ Change in Average Consumer Price Index

6. According to the graph, what happened to the Average Consumer Price Index in the 1970s and 1980s?

   A) It began increasing at an accelerated rate.

   B) It began increasing at a gradual rate.

   C) It stayed constant for consumers.

   D) It remained unchanged until about the 1980s.

7. According to the graph, how has the Average Consumer Price Index changed over time?

   A) It has remained constant.

   B) It has fluctuated, stabilizing toward the end of the century and the early 2000s.

   C) It was stable in the early twentieth century, but it became unstable in the early 2000s.

   D) It has been unstable since the early twentieth century.

8. According to the text and graph, have prices in the United States increased or decreased since the mid-1980s?

   A) Prices have increased.

   B) Prices have decreased.

   C) Prices have remained constant.

   D) There is not enough information to answer the question.

9. Considering the information shown in the graph, what is the MOST likely outcome for the Average Consumer Price Index in the future, if current trends continue?

   A) It will stabilize.

   B) It will fluctuate.

   C) It will continue decreasing.

   D) It will continue increasing.

10. Would a refrigerator be more expensive in 2010 than it was in 1930?

   A) Yes, a refrigerator would be more expensive in 2010 than it was in 1930.

   B) No, a refrigerator would be more expensive in 1930.

   C) Refrigerators would cost about the same in 1930 and 2010.

   D) There is not enough information to answer this question.

Questions 11 – 14 are about this map of a state park.

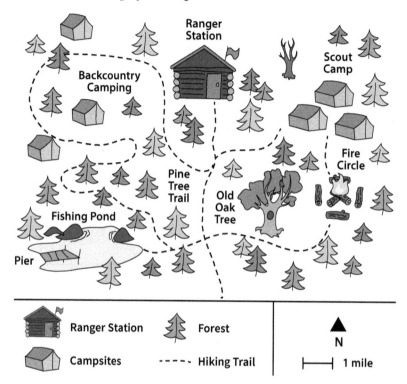

11. Which of the following is located due north of the Fire Circle?

   A) Old Oak Tree

   B) Scout Camp

   C) Fishing Pond

   D) Backcountry Camping

12. If a camper followed the trail from the Fishing Pond to the Scout Camp and passed by the Fire Circle, which of the following would she also have to pass by?

   A) Old Oak Tree

   B) Ranger Station

   C) Backcountry Camping

   D) Pier

13. Which of the following is located due south to southwest of the Backcountry Camping area?

   A) Old Oak Tree

   B) Scout Camp

   C) Fishing Pond

   D) Ranger Station

14. If a camper followed the trail from the Fire Circle to the Pier and passed by the Old Oak Tree, in which direction would he MOSTLY need to walk?

   A) north

   B) south

   C) east

   D) west

East River High School has released its graduation summary for the class of 2016. Out of a total of 558 senior students, 525 (94 percent) successfully completed their degree program and graduated. Of these, 402 (representing 72 percent of the total class) went on to attend to a two- or four-year college or university. The distribution of students among the four main types of colleges and universities—small or large private and small or large public—is shown in the figure below. As the data shows, the majority of East River High School's college-attending graduates chose a large, public institution.

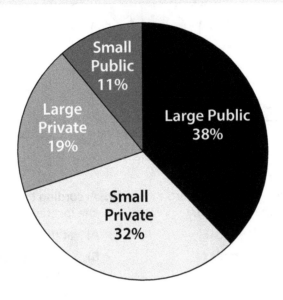

15. According to the passage and the pie graph, about how many students from East River High School will attend a small, public college or university?

    A) 4

    B) 44

    C) 440

    D) 4,400

16. According to the passage and the pie graph, about how many students from East River High School will attend a small, private college or university?

    A) 9

    B) 29

    C) 129

    D) 1,290

17. According to the passage and the pie graph, what percentage of the students from East River High School will attend public colleges or universities (as opposed to private ones)?

    A) 4.9 percent

    B) 49 percent

    C) 5.1 percent

    D) 51 percent

The diagram below represents the lock and key model of enzymes. Questions 18 and 19 ask about this diagram.

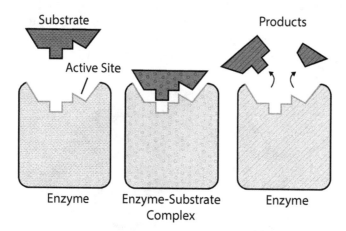

18. According to the figure, the products are formed from which of the following?

A) the enzyme

B) the enzyme-substrate complex

C) the substrate

D) the active site

19. According to the figure, where is the active site located?

A) at the top of the enzyme

B) on the bottom of the enzyme-substrate complex

C) at the top of the substrate

D) in the middle of the products

Questions 20 and 21 are about this graph, which depicts temperatures from January to July.

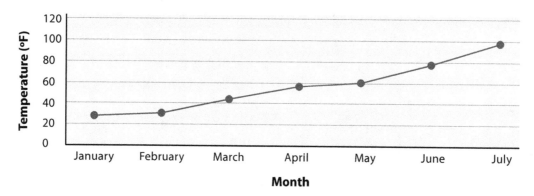

20. According to the line graph, about how many degrees Fahrenheit did the average temperature rise between January and July?

A) about 25 degrees

B) about 50 degrees

C) about 75 degrees

D) about 100 degrees

21. According to the line graph, about how many degrees warmer was it in June than it was in April?

A) 10 degrees warmer

B) 20 degrees warmer

C) 30 degrees warmer

D) 40 degrees warmer

Review this map of downtown Springville. Then, answer the following questions.

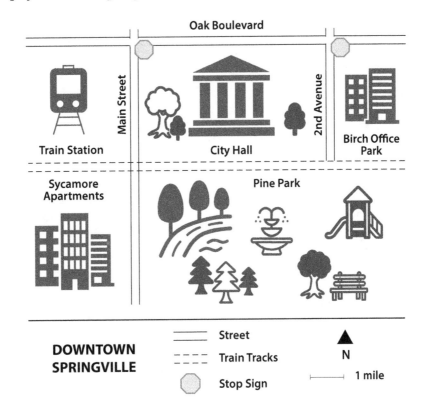

DOWNTOWN SPRINGVILLE

Street

Train Tracks

Stop Sign

N

1 mile

22. A family leaves the train station and heads south on Main Street. At which of the following locations will the family arrive?

A) City Hall

B) Oak Boulevard

C) Sycamore Apartments

D) Birch Office Park

23. According to the map, which of the following is the distance from City Hall to the Birch Office Park?

A) 0.5 miles

B) 2.5 miles

C) 5 miles

D) 10 miles

24. According to the map, which of the following is the distance from the Train Station to the Birch Office Park?

A) 0.5 miles

B) 1 mile

C) 7 miles

D) 49 miles

25. A woman leaves the Sycamore Apartments and drives to her workplace in the Birch Office Park. Which route does she take?

A) She drives north on 2nd Avenue, turns left onto Oak Boulevard, and then turns left onto Main Street.

B) She drives east on Oak Boulevard and turns right onto Main Street.

C) She drives west on Oak Boulevard and turns left onto Main Street.

D) She drives north on Main Street, turns right on Oak Boulevard, and then turns right onto 2nd Avenue.

The following questions are about this graph, comparing class test scores and homework scores over several weeks.

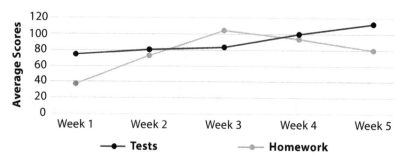

26. According to the line graph, about how many points did average test scores rise between Week 1 and Week 5?

A) about 7 points

B) about 17 points

C) about 27 points

D) about 37 points

27. According to the line graph, about how many points did average homework scores rise between Week 1 and Week 3?

A) about 44 points

B) about 54 points

C) about 64 points

D) about 74 points

Review the diagram of Earth's layers. Then, answer the questions.

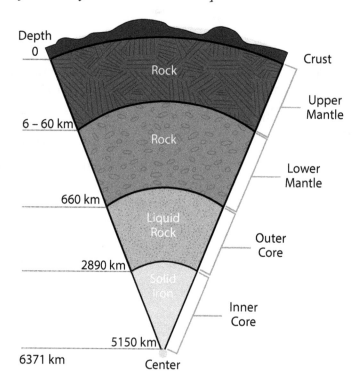

28. According to the diagram, what is at the earth's inner core?

A) solid rock

B) liquid rock

C) solid iron

D) a crust

29. According to the diagram, how deep is the deepest portion of the earth's lower mantle?

A) 0 km

B) 60 km

C) 660 km

D) 2890 km

Questions 30 – 34 refer to this diagram about the checks and balances of the US government.

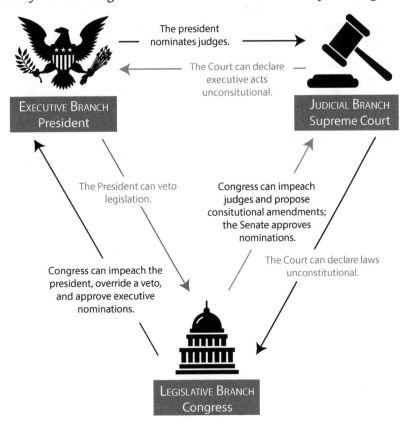

30. According to the figure, how can the executive branch of the US government "check" (take power away from) the legislative branch?

   A) Congress can impeach the president, override a veto, and approve executive nominations.

   B) The president can veto legislation.

   C) The president nominates judges.

   D) Congress can impeach judges and propose constitutional amendments; the Senate approves nominations.

31. According to the figure, how can the judicial branch of the US government "check" (take power away from) the legislative branch?

   A) The Supreme Court can declare a president's orders unconstitutional.

   B) The president nominates judges.

   C) The Supreme Court can declare laws unconstitutional.

   D) Congress can impeach judges and propose constitutional amendments; the Senate approves nominations.

32. According to the figure, which branch of the US government is the MOST powerful?

   A) the executive branch

   B) the legislative branch

   C) the judicial branch

   D) Theoretically, they are equally powerful.

33. According to the figure, which TWO powers are executive powers?

   A) the power to make laws and the power to declare laws unconstitutional

   B) the power to veto laws and the power to nominate judges

   C) the power to declare laws unconstitutional and the power to nominate judges

   D) the power to make laws and the power to veto laws

34. According to the figure, how can the legislative branch of the US government "check" (take power away from) the executive branch?

   A) Congress can impeach the president, override a veto, and approve executive nominations.

   B) The president can veto legislation.

   C) The president nominates judges.

   D) Congress can impeach judges and propose constitutional amendments; the Senate approves nominations.

Review the figure, which depicts a thermometer. Then, answer the following questions.

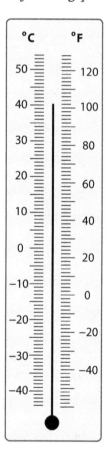

35. Which of the following represents the temperature in degrees Fahrenheit (F) according to the thermometer?

   A) 41

   B) 42

   C) 101

   D) 102

36. Which of the following represents the temperature in degrees Celsius (C) according to the thermometer?

   A) 41

   B) 42

   C) 101

   D) 102

Questions 37 and 38 are about the graph below, depicting ice cream consumption at summer camp.

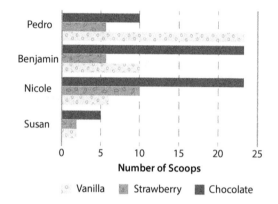

37. According to the bar graph, which two campers ate the most chocolate ice cream during a three-week session at summer camp?

   A) Pedro and Benjamin

   B) Pedro and Nicole

   C) Nicole and Susan

   D) Benjamin and Nicole

38. According to the bar graph, which camper seems to like vanilla ice cream more than the other three do?

   A) Benjamin

   B) Nicole

   C) Pedro

   D) Susan

WORKPLACE DOCUMENTS

Passage One

The following questions refer to this passage from the US Equal Employment Opportunity Commission website.

Under the laws enforced by EEOC, it is illegal to discriminate against someone (applicant or employee) because of that person's race, color, religion, sex (including gender identity, sexual orientation, and pregnancy), national origin, age (40 or older), disability, or genetic information. It is also illegal to retaliate against a person because he or she complained about discrimination, filed a charge of discrimination, or participated in an employment discrimination investigation or lawsuit.

The law forbids discrimination in every aspect of employment.

The laws enforced by EEOC prohibit an employer or other covered entity from using neutral employment policies and practices that have a disproportionately negative effect on applicants or employees of a particular race, color, religion, sex (including gender identity, sexual orientation, and pregnancy), or national origin, or on an individual with a disability or class of individuals with disabilities, if the policies or practices at issue are not job-related and necessary to the operation of the business. The laws enforced by EEOC also prohibit an employer from using neutral employment policies and practices that have a disproportionately negative impact on applicants or employees age 40 or older, if the policies or practices at issue are not based on a reasonable factor other than age.

1. According to the passage, an employer could legally reject a job applicant for which reason?

   A) The applicant is Asian American.

   B) The applicant did not graduate from high school.

   C) The applicant is a person of color.

   D) The applicant is Jewish rather than Christian.

   E) The applicant is a woman rather than a man.

2. According to the passage, an employer could be sued for violating the EEOC for discriminating against which of the following people?

   A) an office worker who became pregnant

   B) an office worker who stole money from the company

   C) an office worker who cannot get along with coworkers

   D) a restaurant server who is consistently rude to customers

   E) a restaurant cook whose work visa expired

3. According to the passage, an employer can legally reject a job applicant if the applicant

   A) is openly gay.

   B) filed a discrimination lawsuit against a former employer.

   C) has a disability that prevents them from performing the job duties.

   D) is over forty years old.

   E) is over fifty years old.

4. According to the passage, an employer could be sued for violating the EEOC for what reason?

   A) laying off workers because the employer can no longer afford to pay them

   B) giving only one out of ten workers a raise

   C) asking workers to work overtime to meet a deadline

   D) firing a worker because she is transgender

   E) firing a worker because he violates company rules

5. According to the passage, how does the EEOC help workers who file discrimination lawsuits?

   A) The EEOC pays for workers' attorneys.

   B) The EEOC pays damages to workers who experience discrimination in the workplace.

   C) The EEOC prevents an employer from firing a worker who files a discrimination lawsuit.

   D) The EEOC provides free counseling to workers who feel stressed out at work.

   E) The EEOC closes businesses whose owners have discriminated against their workers.

Passage Two

The following questions refer to this passage from the US Department of Agriculture website. This section addresses issues Americans face when traveling with their pets within and outside the United States.

TRAVEL WITH YOUR PET STATE TO STATE (INTERSTATE)

When traveling with your pet(s), there may be animal health requirements specific for that destination. As soon as you know your travel details, contact your local veterinarian to assist with the pet travel process. Factors to consider may include meeting time frames for obtaining a health certificate, updating vaccinations, diagnostic testing, or administration of medications/treatments.

BRING YOUR PET INTO THE UNITED STATES FROM A FOREIGN COUNTRY (IMPORT)

[...]

Animals entering the US may be subject to regulation by the US Department of Agriculture Animal and Plant Health Inspection Service (USDA APHIS) as well as other federal agencies. Depending on your destination state, your pet may need to also meet additional health requirements.

- It is the responsibility of the pet owner to make sure their pet has met the entry requirements of the US. Failure to meet these import requirements will result in problems upon arrival in the US.

- Multiple agencies may have regulatory authority over your pet when it enters the US. It is important to notify and coordinate with all responsible government agencies. Contact information and additional details are located on each specific pet page.

- If you need clarification of the entry requirements, please contact the National Import Export Services by phone at (301) 851-3300 or email.

6. According to the passage, whom should a pet owner contact to "assist with the pet travel process"?

   A) a veterinary hospital located at the travel destination

   B) the National Import Export Services at the phone number provided

   C) the pet owner's local veterinarian

   D) the airline on which the pet owner and pet will travel

   E) the State Department of the United States of America

7. What situation does the passage cover besides interstate (state-to-state) travel with a pet?

   A) interstate travel with a farm animal

   B) locating a new veterinarian after moving to a new home

   C) bringing farm animal(s) into the United States from a foreign country

   D) bringing pet(s) into the United States from a foreign country

   E) shipboard regulations for traveling with a service animal on a cruise

8. According to the passage, what does the phrase "meeting time frames" refer to?

   A) allowing plenty of time to take a pet through customs on arrival in the United States

   B) meeting required deadlines for processes such as obtaining health certificates, updating vaccinations, and so on

   C) being on time for every appointment with your local veterinarian

   D) allowing enough time to call or email every government agency that has "regulatory authority" over pets that enter the United States

   E) allowing plenty of time to take your pet through security checks at airports, train stations, bus depots, and so on

9. According to the passage, why might a pet owner be unable to bring a pet across state lines within the United States?

   A) The pet is too old.

   B) The pet is pregnant.

   C) The pet does not meet health requirements in its home state.

   D) The pet does not meet health requirements in the state it is entering.

   E) The pet is originally from a foreign country.

10. According to the passage, how many pets may an owner bring into the United States from a foreign country?

    A) one

    B) two

    C) three

    D) four

    E) The passage does not specify a limit.

11. What kinds of animals does the passage MOST LIKELY cover?

    A) pets and farm animals

    B) pets and zoo animals

    C) endangered animals

    D) pets only

    E) dogs and cats only

12. Judging from the passage, which is the best motto for people who plan to travel with pets?

    A) Live for the moment.

    B) Be prepared.

    C) A dog is man's best friend.

    D) Traveling is like herding cats.

    E) Today is the first day of the rest of your life.

13. The second section of the passage says that "failure to meet these import requirements will result in problems upon arrival in the US." What "problem" does this MOST likely refer to?

    A) The pet owner may not be able to care for the pet adequately.

    B) The pet may have to be euthanized immediately upon arrival in the United States.

    C) The pet may have to be sent back to its country of origin without its owner.

    D) The owner may be arrested and jailed for failing to "meet … import requirements."

    E) Animal control authorities may keep the pet until its owner "meet[s] … import requirements."

14. The second section of the passage says that "multiple agencies may have regulatory authority over your pet when it enters the US." Why is it important for a pet owner to be aware of this fact?

    A) The owner may have to meet more than one set of government regulations in order to "import" pet(s).

    B) Large states such as California make it especially difficult for owners to "import" pet(s).

    C) States with many farm animals are especially strict when it comes to "importing" farm animals and poultry from foreign countries.

    D) Most US city governments do not allow pet owners to "import" exotic pet(s).

    E) In farming states such as Idaho, county sheriffs have the authority to decide whether an animal owner may "import" animals from foreign countries.

15. According to the passage, when should a pet owner begin researching and taking steps in "the pet travel process"?

   A) on the day of departure

   B) upon arrival at the travel destination

   C) about one year before traveling

   D) about one month before traveling

   E) as soon as the owner knows their "travel details"

Passage Three

The following questions refer to this passage that discusses regulations on youth employment, from the US Department of Labor website.

The Department of Labor is the sole federal agency that monitors child labor and enforces child labor laws. The most sweeping federal law that restricts the employment and abuse of child workers is the Fair Labor Standards Act (FLSA). Child labor provisions under FLSA are designed to protect the educational opportunities of youth and prohibit their employment in jobs that are detrimental to their health and safety. FLSA restricts the hours that youth under 16 years of age can work and lists hazardous occupations too dangerous for young workers to perform. Enforcement of the FLSA's child labor provisions is handled by the Department's Wage and Hour Division.

The Office of Disability Employment Policy (ODEP) offers numerous resources for youth. ODEP's focus on youth policy is aimed at improving transition outcomes of youth and young adults with disabilities toward successful employment and adulthood.

The Department's YouthRules! initiative seeks to promote positive and safe work experiences for young workers.

The Employment and Training Administration sponsors many programs designed to provide training opportunities and job placement assistance programs for America's youth.

16. What is the main idea of the passage?

   A) The Department of Labor was created to monitor child labor.

   B) The Fair Labor Standards Act (FLSA) restricts the employment and abuse of child workers.

   C) Several different agencies and laws deal with child and youth employment in the United States.

   D) In the United States, children under sixteen may not work long hours at dangerous jobs.

   E) The US government tries to support teens over sixteen who wish to work so they can earn money.

17. How might the FLSA "protect the educational opportunities" of children and young people? Choose the MOST likely answer.

   A) by donating money to public and private schools throughout the United States

   B) by preventing children under sixteen from working long hours

   C) by creating educational programs that teach job skills to teens

   D) by making it unlawful for children to work in family businesses

   E) by encouraging teachers to act as job counselors for their students

18. According to the passage, who are the main beneficiaries of ODEP?

A) children under sixteen

B) youths and young adults with disabilities

C) parents who want their children to develop job skills

D) employers who cannot afford to pay more than minimum wage

E) children and youths with good ideas for small businesses

19. According to the passage, what is the focus of the Labor Department's YouthRules! initiative?

A) to teach young workers how to become managers in stores and restaurants

B) to help young workers develop their résumés and practice interviewing for jobs

C) to promote safe and positive work experiences for young workers

D) to teach young workers about health regulations in food-related businesses

E) to find higher-paying jobs for young workers who wish to supplement family income

20. According to the passage, what does the Employment and Training Administration do for young people in the US, in addition to providing training opportunities?

A) It funds part-time jobs in the federal government.

B) It prevents children under sixteen from working long hours.

C) It encourages schoolchildren to research career paths.

D) It provides job placement assistance.

E) It supports raising the minimum wage.

Passage Four

The following questions refer to this excerpt from a letter to college and university presidents from the US Department of Justice and the US Department of Education.

Dear College or University President:

We write to express concern on the part of the Department of Justice and the Department of Education that colleges and universities are using electronic book readers that are not accessible to students who are blind or have low vision and to seek your help in ensuring that this emerging technology is used in classroom settings in a manner that is permissible under federal law. A serious problem with some of these devices is that they lack an accessible text-to-speech function. Requiring use of an emerging technology in a classroom environment when the technology is inaccessible to an entire population of individuals with disabilities—individuals with visual disabilities—is discrimination prohibited by the Americans with Disabilities Act of 1990 (ADA) and Section 504 of the Rehabilitation Act of 1973 (Section 504) unless those individuals are provided accommodations or modifications that permit them to receive all the educational benefits provided by the technology in an equally effective and equally integrated manner.

The Departments of Justice and Education share responsibility for protecting the rights of college and university students with disabilities. The Department of Justice is responsible for enforcement and implementation of title III of the ADA, which covers private colleges and universities, and the Departments of Justice and Education both have enforcement authority under title II of the ADA, which covers public universities. In addition, the Department of Education enforces Section 504 with respect to public and private colleges and universities that receive federal financial assistance from the Department of

Education. As discussed below, the general requirements of Section 504 and the ADA reach equipment and technological devices when they are used by public entities or places of public accommodation as part of their programs, services, activities, goods, advantages, privileges, or accommodations.

Technology is the hallmark of the future, and technological competency is essential to preparing all students for future success. Emerging technologies are an educational resource that enhances the experience for everyone, and perhaps especially for students with disabilities. Technological innovations have opened a virtual world of commerce, information, and education to many individuals with disabilities for whom access to the physical world remains challenging. Ensuring equal access to emerging technology in university and college classrooms is a means to the goal of full integration and equal educational opportunity for this nation's students with disabilities. With technological advances, procuring electronic book readers that are accessible should be neither costly nor difficult.

We appreciate your consideration of this essential educational issue and look forward to working with you to ensure that our nation's colleges and universities are fully accessible to individuals with disabilities.

21. What is the letter's main purpose?

- **A)** to encourage colleges and universities to enroll more students with disabilities
- **B)** to criticize college and university officials who discriminate against students with disabilities
- **C)** to show that educational technology can be very helpful to college and university students with varying disabilities
- **D)** to make electronic book readers used in colleges and universities accessible to students with visual disabilities
- **E)** to make electronic book readers used in colleges and universities accessible to students who are deaf

22. According to the letter, what law(s) does the phrase "permissible under federal law" refer to?

- **A)** various state and local laws that cover college and university students with disabilities
- **B)** the Constitution of the United States of America
- **C)** the Americans with Disabilities Act of 1990 (ADA) and Section 504 of the Rehabilitation Act of 1973
- **D)** the federal Bill of Rights, which covers freedom of speech, freedom of the press, and other rights
- **E)** various Supreme Court decisions pertaining to college and university students with disabilities

23. Who MOST likely wrote this letter?

- **A)** college and university presidents throughout the United States
- **B)** officials at the US Department of Justice and the US Department of Education
- **C)** college and university students with disabilities
- **D)** manufacturers and sellers of electronic book readers
- **E)** college and university students who are blind or deaf, or who have speech impediments

24. According to the letter, what would fix the discriminatory situation the writers are addressing?

- **A)** finding out whether electronic book readers used in colleges and universities include accessible text-to-speech functions
- **B)** pointing out that most electronic book readers used in colleges and universities lack accessible text-to-speech functions
- **C)** discontinuing the use of electronic book readers in colleges and universities
- **D)** demanding that manufacturers invent accessible text-to-speech functions for electronic book readers
- **E)** making sure that all electronic book readers used in colleges and universities *do* include accessible text-to-speech functions

25. Which paragraph in the letter both states a problem and proposes a solution?

- **A)** the first paragraph
- **B)** the second paragraph
- **C)** the third paragraph
- **D)** the fourth paragraph
- **E)** None of the paragraphs do both.

26. What levels of education does the letter MOST likely cover?

- **A)** kindergarten through eighth grade
- **B)** high school and college
- **C)** college and graduate school
- **D)** elementary school only
- **E)** middle school and high school

27. Why do the writers include the phrase "technology is the hallmark of the future"? Choose the MOST likely response.

- **A)** to predict that the future will be much better than the present
- **B)** to impress college and university presidents with educated-sounding rhetoric
- **C)** to criticize the past and the present by praising the future
- **D)** to criticize those who discriminate against students with disabilities
- **E)** to emphasize that everyone deserves equal access to technology

28. Which of the following phrases BEST describes the letter's tone?

- **A)** concerned, critical, and pessimistic
- **B)** critical, threatening, and businesslike
- **C)** concerned, supportive, and optimistic
- **D)** excited, enthusiastic, and joyful
- **E)** distracted, unconcerned, yet persuasive

29. In the third paragraph, how do the writers explain the idea that "emerging technologies are an educational resource that enhances the experience for everyone, and perhaps especially for students with disabilities"?

- **A)** by saying that it is unfair to exclude students with disabilities from participating fully
- **B)** by pointing out that "emerging technologies" are especially helpful to disabled students
- **C)** by explaining that students without visual disabilities can read in a traditional manner—by reading hardcopy books
- **D)** by using a critical or pessimistic tone rather than an upbeat, hopeful tone
- **E)** by citing concrete examples of blind students who were able to use electronic book readers

30. Which of the following phrases do the writers use to persuade college and university presidents to provide accessible electronic book readers?

- **A)** "in classroom settings" (paragraph 1)
- **B)** "an emerging technology" (paragraph 1)
- **C)** "for enforcement and implementation" (paragraph 2)
- **D)** "neither costly nor difficult" (paragraph 3)
- **E)** "accessible to individuals" (paragraph 4)

Passage Five

The following questions refer to this excerpt from the Americans with Disabilities Act (ADA) Standards, which discusses making plumbing facilities accessible to all Americans.

CHAPTER 6: PLUMBING ELEMENTS AND FACILITIES

602 Drinking Fountains

602.1 General. Drinking fountains shall comply with 307 and 602.

602.2 Clear Floor Space. Units shall have a clear floor or ground space complying with 305 positioned for a forward approach and centered on the unit. Knee and toe clearance complying with 306 shall be provided.

EXCEPTION: A parallel approach complying with 305 shall be permitted at units for children's use where the spout is 30 inches (760 mm) maximum above the finish floor or ground and is 3½ inches (90 mm) maximum from the front edge of the unit, including bumpers.

602.3 Operable Parts. Operable parts shall comply with 309.

602.4 Spout Height. Spout outlets shall be 36 inches (915 mm) maximum above the finish floor or ground.

602.5 Spout Location. The spout shall be located 15 inches (380 mm) minimum from the vertical support and 5 inches (125 mm) maximum from the front edge of the unit, including bumpers.

31. What is the topic of Chapter 6?
    A) drinking fountains for adults with disabilities
    B) plumbing elements and facilities for people with disabilities
    C) floor space under and near drinking fountains
    D) drinking fountains for children
    E) drinking fountains' spout heights

32. What does section 602.3 describe?
    A) drinking fountains' spout heights
    B) drinking fountains for children's use
    C) drinking fountains' operable parts
    D) drinking fountains' spout locations
    E) toilet stalls for people in wheelchairs

33. The word *bumpers* is mentioned twice in section 602. What does this word MOST likely refer to?
    A) automobile bumpers
    B) bumper cars in theme parks
    C) bumpers on drinking fountains
    D) bumpers between boats and docks
    E) bumpers on toilet stall walls and doors

34. According to the passage, how high above the finish floor or ground must drinking fountains' spout outlets be?
    A) 5 inches maximum
    B) 15 inches minimum
    C) 36 inches maximum
    D) 380 mm minimum
    E) 1,016 mm maximum

35. What does the phrase "shall comply with" MOST LIKELY mean, in the context of the passage?
    A) must submit architectural plans
    B) must fulfill clients' needs and desires
    C) must follow the rules listed under
    D) must obey the supervisor's orders
    E) must observe certain customs

ANSWER KEY

APPLIED MATHEMATICS

1. **D) is correct.** Write a proportion and then solve for x.
$$\frac{40}{45} = \frac{265}{x}$$
$$40x = 11,925$$
$$x = 298.125 \approx \textbf{298}$$

2. **C) is correct.** Use the formula for percent change.
$$percent\ change = \frac{amount\ of\ change}{original\ amount}$$
$$= \frac{(7,375 - 7,250)}{7,250} = 0.017 = \textbf{1.7\%}$$

3. **A) is correct.** Evaluate to find the greatest value.
$$20 - (-20) = \textbf{40}$$
$$-16 - 17 + 31 = -2$$
$$18 - 15 + 27 = 30$$
$$-20 + 10 + 10 = 0$$
$$-4(3)(-2) = 24$$

4. **E) is correct.** Make the exponents the same and subtract the digit parts of each term.
$$(4.71 \times 10^3) - (2.98 \times 10^2)$$
$$4.71 \times 10 \times 10^2 = 47.1 \times 10^2$$
$$47.1 - 2.98 = 44.12$$
$$44.12 \times 10^2 = \textbf{4.412} \times \textbf{10}^\textbf{3}$$

5. **B) is correct.** Multiply the digits and add the exponents.
$$(1.2 \times 10^{-3})\ (1.13 \times 10^{-4})$$
$$1.2 \times 1.13 = 1.356$$
$$-3 + (-4) = -7$$
$$\textbf{1.356} \times \textbf{10}^{\textbf{-7}}$$

6. **D) is correct.** Simplify using PEMDAS.
$$-(3^2) + (5 - 7)^2 - 3(4 - 8)$$
$$= -(3^2) + (-2)^2 - 3(-4)$$
$$= -9 + 4 - 3(-4)$$
$$= -9 + 4 + 12 = \textbf{7}$$

7. **E) is correct.** Simplify using PEMDAS.
$$(3^2 \div 1^3) - (4 - 8^2) + 2^4$$
$$= (9 \div 1) - (4 - 64) + 16$$
$$= 9 - (-60) + 16 = \textbf{85}$$

8. **B) is correct.** Align the decimals and add/subtract from left to right.
$$17.38 - 19.26 + 14.2$$
$$= (-1.88) + 14.2 = \textbf{12.32}$$

9. **C) is correct.** Convert each fraction to the LCD and subtract the numerators.
$$\frac{7}{8} - \frac{1}{10} - \frac{2}{3}$$
$$= \frac{7}{8}\left(\frac{15}{15}\right) - \frac{1}{10}\left(\frac{12}{12}\right) - \frac{2}{3}\left(\frac{40}{40}\right)$$

$$= \frac{105}{120} - \frac{12}{120} - \frac{80}{120} = \mathbf{\frac{13}{120}}$$

10. **B) is correct.** Convert each term to an improper fraction and multiple/divide left to right.
$$\left(1\tfrac{1}{2}\right)\left(2\tfrac{2}{3}\right) \div \left(1\tfrac{1}{4}\right)$$
$$1\tfrac{1}{2} = \tfrac{3}{2}$$
$$2\tfrac{2}{3} = \tfrac{8}{3}$$
$$1\tfrac{1}{4} = \tfrac{5}{4}$$
$$\left(\tfrac{3}{2}\right)\left(\tfrac{8}{3}\right) \div \tfrac{5}{4} = \tfrac{16}{5} = \mathbf{3\tfrac{1}{5}}$$

11. **E) is correct.** Place the decimal over 100 and simplify.
$$\frac{28}{100} = \frac{7}{25}$$
$$3.28 = \mathbf{3\tfrac{7}{25}}$$

12. **D) is correct.** Write each value in decimal form and compare.
$-0.95 < 0 < 0.4 < 0.35 < 0.75$
FALSE

$-1 < -0.1 < -0.11 < 0.8\overline{3} < 0.75$
FALSE

$-0.75 < -0.2 < 0 < 0.\overline{66} < 0.55$
FALSE

$-1.1 < -0.8 < -0.13 < 0.7 < 0.8\overline{1}$
TRUE

$-0.0001 < -0.\overline{83} < 0 < 0.\overline{66} < 0.8$
FALSE

13. **A) is correct.** Multiply by the converstion factor to get from pounds to kilograms.
8 pounds, 8 ounces = 8.5 pounds
$$8.5 \text{ lb.} \left(\frac{1 \text{ kg}}{2.2 \text{ lb.}}\right) = \mathbf{3.9 \text{ kg}}$$

14. **B) is correct.** Find the highest possible multiple of 4 that is less than or equal to 397, and then subtract to find the remainder.
$99 \times 4 = 396$
$397 - 396 = \mathbf{1}$

15. **A) is correct.** The 8 is in the thousands place. Because the value to the right of the 8 is less than 5, the 8 remains the same and all values to its right become zero. The result is **498,000.**

16. **A) is correct.** Add the fractions and subtract the result from the amount of flour Allison started with.
$$2\tfrac{1}{2} + \tfrac{3}{4} = \tfrac{5}{2} + \tfrac{3}{4} = \tfrac{10}{4} + \tfrac{3}{4} = \tfrac{13}{4}$$
$$4 - \tfrac{13}{4} = \tfrac{16}{4} - \tfrac{13}{4} = \mathbf{\tfrac{3}{4}}$$

17. **A) is correct.** Add the number of cupcakes he will give to his friend and to his coworkers, then subtract that value from 48.
# of cupcakes for his friend:
$$\tfrac{1}{2} \times 48 = 24$$
# of cupcakes for his coworkers:
$$\tfrac{1}{3} \times 48 = 16$$
$$48 - (24 + 16) = \mathbf{8}$$

18. **D) is correct.** To estimate the amount of the change, round the price of each item to the nearest dollar amount and subtract from the total.
$\$50 - (\$13 + \$12 + \$4 + \$6)$
$= \$50 - \$35 = \mathbf{\$15}$

19. **B) is correct.** There are 15 minutes between 7:45 a.m. and 8:00 a.m. and 20 minutes between 8:00 a.m. and 8:20 a.m.
15 minutes + 20 minutes =
35 minutes

20. **C) is correct.** Use the formula for finding percentages. Express the percentage as a decimal.
part = whole × percentage = **1560 × 0.15**

21. **E) is correct.** Use the formula for percent increase.
$$percent\ increase = \frac{amount\ of\ change}{original\ amount}$$
$$= \frac{3{,}000}{57{,}000} = 0.0526 \approx \mathbf{5\%}$$

22. **D) is correct.** Set up a proportion and solve.
$$\frac{8}{650} = \frac{12}{x}$$
$$12(650) = 8x$$
$$\mathbf{\mathit{x} = 975\ miles}$$

23. **B) is correct.** Multiply the cost per pounds by the number of pounds purchased to find the cost of each fruit.

apples: 2(1.89) = 3.78

oranges: 1.5(2.19) = 3.285

3.78 + 3.285 = 7.065 = **$7.07**

24. **D) is correct.** Set up an equation. The original price (p) minus 30% of the original price is $385.

$p - 0.3p = 385$

$p = \frac{385}{0.7} = $ **$550**

25. **D) is correct.**

{5, 11, 18, 20, **37**, 37, 60, 72, 90}

median = 37

mode = 37

$mean = \frac{60 + 5 + 18 + 20 + 37 + 37 + 11 + 90 + 72}{9}$

= 38.89

The median is less than the mean.

26. **D) is correct.** The probability of getting a room without an ocean view is equal to 1 minus the probability of getting a room with an ocean view.

$P_{view} = 1 - P_{no\ ocean\ view}$

$P_{view} = 1 - 0.35 = 0.65$

Use the equation for percentages to find the number of rooms without a view.

part = percentage × whole= (0.65)400 = **260 rooms**

27. **B) is correct.** In 2012, New York had more months with less than 3 inches of rain than either Chicago or Houston.

28. **E) is correct.** Use the graph to find the number of months Chicago had less than 3 inches of rain year, and then find the average.

months with < 3 inches rain in Chicago:

{7, 8, 10, 7, 9, 10, 10}

$\frac{(7 + 8 + 10 + 7 + 9 + 10 + 10)}{7} = 8.7 \approx$ **9**

29. **C) is correct.** Use the formula for percent change.

$percent\ change = \frac{amount\ of\ change}{original\ amount}$

= (680 − 425) / 425

= 255/425 = 0.60 = **60%**

30. **A) is correct.** Find the amount the state will spend on infrastructure and education, and then find the difference.

infrastructure = 0.2(3,000,000,000) = 600,000,000

education = 0.18(3,000,000,000) = 540,000,000

600,000,000 − 540,000,000 = **$60,000,000**

31. **A) Correct.** Twenty-five students earned an F in science, and 70 students earned an A in science; 2(25) < 70.

B. Incorrect. There are 170 total students with math grades. A majority would be more than half (85). Only 25 students earned a C in math.

C. Incorrect. Forty students earned a B in reading and 35 students earned a B in math.

D. Incorrect. The graph does not include information about next year's students.

E. Incorrect. The same number of students (25) earned C's and D's in science.

32. **D) is correct.** Find the area of the square as if it did not have the corners cut out.

12 mm × 12 mm = 144 mm²

Find the area of the four cut out corners.

2 mm × 2 mm = 4 mm²

4(4 mm²) = 16 mm²

Subtract the area of the cut out corners from the large square to find the area of the shape.

144 mm² − 16 mm² = **128 mm²**

33. **D) is correct.** One way to find the answer is to draw a picture.

Put 24 cans into groups of 4. One out of every 4 cans is diet (light gray) so there is 1 light gray can for every 3 dark gray cans.

That leaves 18 dark gray cans (regular soda).

Alternatively, solve the problem using ratios.

$$\frac{Regular}{Total} = \frac{3}{4} = \frac{x}{24}$$

$$4x = 72$$

$$x = 18$$

34. B) is correct. Add the base amount and the tax on the extra percentage of the person's income.

GRAPHIC LITERACY

1. **A) is correct.** The systolic blood pressure, 152, is the number marked as "SYS" on the monitor.

2. **B) is correct.** The diastolic blood pressure, 95, is the number marked as "DIA" on the monitor.

3. **C) is correct.** The pulse, 98, is the number marked as "PULSE" on the monitor.

4. **B) is correct.** In February the service earned $1,000, and in April it earned $200. The difference between the two months is $800.

5. **A) is correct.** In February the service earned about $1,000, and in March it earned about $500. The combined February/March amount was about $1,500. In January the service earned about $800, in April it earned about $200, and in May it earned almost $400. The combined January/April/May amount was about $1,400. About $1,400 is about $100 less than about $1,500.

6. **A) is correct.** The dark line that measures the Average Consumer Price Index takes a steep turn upward in the 1970s. That indicates that the Average Consumer Price Index began to quickly increase during that time.

7. **B) is correct.** The gray line that depicts change in average CPI fluctuates in the early twentieth century, swinging to a high of 250 then dropping below 50 all before 1920. Throughout the 1920s, the average swings from just above 100 to below 50. In the 1940s, it swings from 100 to above 200. However, from the 1980s onward, the line is mostly stable, aside from a dip after the year 2000.

8. **A) is correct.** The text states that the base year is 1982 – 1984. The Average Consumer Price Index has steadily increased since the mid-1980s. That means prices have risen.

9. **D) is correct.** The graph shows an upward trend in the Average Consumer Price Index, represented by the dark line. It seems likely that it will continue increasing if trends continue.

10. **A) is correct.** The dark line represents the Average Consumer Price Index, which reflects changes in prices over time. In 1930, the Average Consumer Price Index was low in comparison to the "base year" of 1982 – 1984. Since the 1980s, the Average Consumer Price Index has steadily increased. In 2010, the Average Consumer Price Index was 20 percent higher than it was in the mid-1980s, and almost 35 percent higher than it was in the 1930s. Therefore, it can be concluded that prices are higher in 2010 than they were in the early 1930s.

11. **B) is correct.** The Scout Camp is due north of the Fire Circle.

12. **A) is correct.** The Old Oak Tree lies on the trail between the Fishing Pond and the Fire Circle.

13. **C) is correct.** The Fishing Pond is due south to southwest of the Backcountry Camping area.

14. **D) is correct.** The Pier lies west of the Old Oak Tree and the Fire Circle.

15. **B) is correct.** The passage states that 402 students went on to attend college or university, and 11 percent of 402 is approximately 44 students.

16. **C) is correct.** The passage states that 402 students went on to attend college or university, and 32 percent of 402 is approximately 129 students.

17. **B) is correct.** The pie graph shows that 38 percent of the students went on to attend large public institutions, while 11 percent attended small public colleges and universities. Thirty-eight plus 11 equals 49 percent, or about 197 students out of 402.

18. **C) is correct.** The diagram indicates that products are formed when the substrate is broken apart.

19. **A) is correct.** The diagram indicates that the active site is located at the top of the enzyme.

20. **C) is correct.** The line graph shows that in January the average temperature was about 25 degrees Fahrenheit, while in July the average temperature was almost 100 degrees Fahrenheit. The average temperature rose about 75 degrees in the months between January and July.

21. **B) is correct.** The line graph shows that in April the average temperature was almost 60 degrees Fahrenheit, while in June the average temperature was almost 80 degrees Fahrenheit. So, in June it was about 20 degrees warmer than it was in April.

22. **C) is correct.** Of the four choices, only Sycamore Apartments is located on Main Street south of the train station.

23. **B) is correct.** The scale shows that the two buildings are approximately 2.5 miles apart.

24. **B) is correct.** The scale shows that the Birch Office Park is about 7 miles distance from the Train Station.

25. **D) is correct.** Of the four choices, only this route will take the woman from the Sycamore Apartments to the Birch Office Park.

26. **D) is correct.** The line graph shows that during Week 1 the average test score was about 75 points, while during Week 5 the average test score was about 112 points. The average test score rose about 37 points between Week 1 and Week 5.

27. **C) is correct.** The line graph shows that during Week 1 the average homework score was about 38 points, while during Week 3 the average homework score was about 102 points. The average homework score rose about 64 points between Week 1 and Week 3.

28. **C) is correct.** The diagram shows that the earth's inner core is solid iron.

29. **C) is correct.** The diagram shows that the lower mantle (which is under the upper mantle) begins at 6 to 60 km below the earth's surface and ends at 660 km (where the outer core begins).

30. **B) is correct.** The executive branch's (the president's) only way of "checking" the legislative branch is to veto legislation.

31. **C) is orrect.** The judicial branch's (the Supreme Court's) only way of "checking" the legislative branch is to declare laws (which Congress has passed) unconstitutional.

32. **D) is correct.** The US government's system of checks and balances is meant to ensure that the three branches of government "check" one another in order to achieve a balance of power. The framers of the Constitution did not want any one of the three branches to be more powerful than the other two.

33. **B) is correct.** The legislative branch has the power to make laws, and the judicial branch has the power to declare laws unconstitutional. The executive branch

(the president) has the power to veto laws and to nominate judges.

34. **A) is correct.** The legislative branch (Congress) possesses three ways of "checking" the executive branch (the president): impeachment, overriding a veto, and approving executive nominations.

35. **D) is correct.** The thermometer indicates that the temperature is around 102 degrees F (Fahrenheit).

36. **A) is correct.** The thermometer indicates that the temperature is around 41 degrees C (Celsius).

37. **D) is correct.** The bar graph shows that Benjamin and Nicole each ate about 23 scoops of chocolate ice-cream, while Pedro ate 10 scoops and Susan ate only 5 scoops.

38. **C) is correct.** The bar graph shows that Pedro ate about 23 scoops of vanilla ice cream, while Benjamin ate 10 scoops, Nicole ate 6 scoops, and Susan ate only 2 scoops.

Workplace Documents

1. **B) is correct.** The passage does not address education.

2. **A) is correct.** The passage says that it is not legal to discriminate against a woman due to pregnancy. The other reasons would probably not merit a valid lawsuit.

3. **C) is correct.** The passage says that employers may reject a job applicant "if the policies or practices at issue are not job-related and necessary to the operation of the business." This suggests that an employer may legally reject an applicant whose disability renders them unable to perform the job duties. (It should be noted that the EEOC does require employers to provide reasonable accommodation for employees with disabilities. For example, an employer might need to install a ramp to accommodate workers in wheelchairs.)

4. **D) is correct.** The passage says that it is not legal to discriminate against workers because of their gender identities.

5. **C) is correct.** The passage says that it is illegal under the EEOC "to retaliate against a person because he or she complained about discrimination, filed a charge of discrimination, or participated in an employment discrimination investigation or lawsuit."

6. **C) is correct.** The passage says, "When traveling with your pet(s), there may be animal health requirements specific for that destination. As soon as you know your travel details, contact your local veterinarian to assist with the pet travel process."

7. **D) is correct.** The second section of the passage is titled "Bring your pet into the United States from a foreign country (Import)."

8. **B) is correct.** The passage says that "factors to consider may include meeting time frames for obtaining a health certificate, updating vaccinations, diagnostic testing, or administration of medications/treatments."

9. **D) is correct.** The passage says that "when traveling with your pet(s), there may be animal health requirements specific for that destination."

10. **E) is correct.** The passage refers to "pet(s)," but it does not say how many pets an owner may legally bring into the United States.

11. **D) is correct.** The passage does not refer to any kinds or species of animals besides "pets."

12. **B) is correct.** The passage advises people who plan to travel with pets to find out exactly which requirements they will need to meet and to allow plenty of time to meet those requirements before they travel.

13. **E) is correct.** All other choices are either irrelevant or overly harsh. Choice E is most likely since the passage lists many rules but no punishments or dire consequences such as those specified in choices B, C, and D. Choice A does not make good sense as a response to the question.

14. **A) is correct.** This is the only reason that makes good sense, given the context. The passage goes on to say that "it is important to notify and coordinate with all responsible government agencies."

15. **E) is correct.** The passage says that "as soon as [the pet owner knows their] travel details, [they should] contact [a] local veterinarian to assist with the pet travel process."

16. **C) is correct.** The passage describes several agencies, laws, and programs that deal with young workers in the United States.

17. **B) is correct.** The passage says that "child labor provisions under FLSA are designed to protect the educational opportunities of youth and prohibit their employment in jobs that are detrimental to their health and safety." Before these provisions became law, young children could be kept out of school in order to work long hours in factories and other workplaces.

18. **B) is correct.** The passage says that "ODEP's focus on youth policy is aimed at improving transition outcomes of youth and young adults with disabilities toward successful employment and adulthood."

19. **C) is correct.** The passage says that "the Department's YouthRules! initiative seeks to promote positive and safe work experiences for young workers."

20. **D) is correct.** The passage says that "the Employment and Training Administration sponsors many programs designed to provide training opportunities and job placement assistance programs for America's youth."

21. **D) is correct.** The first sentence in the letter says, "We write to express concern … that colleges and universities are using electronic book readers that are not accessible to students who are blind or have low vision and to seek [college and university presidents'] help in ensuring that this emerging technology is used in classroom settings in a manner that is permissible under federal law."

22. **C) is correct.** The third sentence in the letter says, "Requiring use of an emerging technology in a classroom environment when the technology is inaccessible to an entire population of individuals with disabilities—individuals with visual disabilities—is discrimination prohibited by the Americans with Disabilities Act of 1990 (ADA) and Section 504 of the Rehabilitation Act of 1973 (Section 504) unless those individuals are provided accommodations or modifications that permit them to receive all the educational benefits provided by the technology in an equally effective and equally integrated manner."

23. **B) is correct.** The introduction to the letter says it is "from the US Department of Justice and the US Department of Education."

24. **E) is correct.** The second and third sentences in the letter say, "A serious problem with some of [the electronic book readers used in colleges and universities] is that they lack an accessible text-to-speech function. Requiring use of an emerging technology in a classroom environment when the technology is inaccessible to an entire population of individuals with disabilities—individuals with visual disabilities—is discrimination…." Adding an accessible text-to-speech function would resolve this problem.

25. **A) is correct.** The first paragraph points out that it is discriminatory to use electronic book readers that are inaccessible to students with visual disabilities. This paragraph also proposes a solution: replace such devices with ones that have "an accessible text-to-speech function" and are thus accessible to all college and university students.

26. **C) is correct.** The letter is addressed to presidents of colleges and universities. These institutions encompass college (undergraduate school) and graduate school (masters and doctoral programs).

27. **E) is correct.** The letter's main purpose is to convince its recipients to help

all students—including those with disabilities—to gain access to the best technology available. ∎

28. **C) is correct.** The letter writers seem confident that the letter's recipients will quickly agree that (1) a change is clearly necessary; (2) the change can be easily and inexpensively achieved; and (3) Americans are in agreement when it comes to obeying federal laws and ensuring that people with disabilities have the same opportunities as those without disabilities.

29. **B) is correct.** The third paragraph goes on to explain that "technological innovations have opened a virtual world of commerce, information, and education to many individuals with disabilities for whom access to the physical world remains challenging."

30. **D) is correct.** The letter writers seem to believe—or hope—that it will be "neither costly nor difficult" for colleges and universities to obtain electronic book readers that are accessible to students who are blind or have low vision. The writers hope that pointing this out will encourage the letter's recipients to make the desired change right away.

31. **B) is correct.** The title of Chapter 6 is "Plumbing Elements and Facilities." Only part of Chapter 6 (section 602) concerns drinking fountains for people with disabilities.

32. **C) is correct.** The heading "Operable Parts" follows the number 602.3.

33. **C) is correct.** Section 602 is about drinking fountains for people with disabilities. The word bumpers most likely refers to spacers or buffers between drinking fountains and wheelchairs.

34. **C) is correct.** Section 602.4 says that "spout outlets shall be 36 inches (915 mm) maximum above the finish floor or ground."

35. **C) is correct.** The passage says, "drinking fountains shall comply with 307 and 602," which means that builders must create drinking fountains according to the rules and specifications listed in sections 307 and 602.

Follow the link below to take your second practice test and to access other online study resources:

www.triviumtestprep.com/act-workkeys-online-resources

CPSIA information can be obtained
at www.ICGtesting.com
Printed in the USA
BVHW061452180123
656522BV00004B/214